Creatively
Ever After
A PATH TO
INNOVATION

Praise For Creatively Ever After

"Clear and concise, this book is a delightful read. Through stories and deliberate strategies, opportunities are provided to expand your thinking and problem solving. Appropriate for professionals to consider multiple angles to get to the heart of effective creative problem solving and for challenging young adults to expand their thinking deliberately."

Susan Keller-Mathers, Ed.D, Associate Professor,
International Center for Studies in Creativity

"A must read for leaders, team members and facilitators who want to free their thinking to create new futures. Easy to relate to, a gentle progression, and great examples. Takes the reader on a unique journey inside the creative problem solving process from start to happy ending using well-known nursery rhyme characters as protagonists."

Marci Segal, President, CreativityLand Inc.

"For a book that is less than 200 pages, Creatively Ever After is big on value. I did not want to put it down! The power of this book is that you can launch a problem solving strategy, making the most of the human intellect, in the smallest period of time, to achieve a goal. The techniques are easy enough to use with children, yet advanced enough for top executives of global companies. Genius!"

Michael Ng, CCH Account Manager

"Creativity Ever After offers a clever and unique take on the Creative Problem Solving process and is incredibly engaging and deceptively simplistic in its approach.,,the reader is encouraged to tap into some of the greatest tools of creativity—humor and playfulness. Appropriate for CPS newbies and experienced practitioners alike, the book provides an easy and approachable means to learn, practice and/or teach CPS. A thoroughly enjoyable journey and a must-read for anyone interested in creative problem solving... one word of caution though—be prepared to laugh out loud!"

Tania Plascencia, Innovation Facilitator, TNS

Creatively Ever After

A PATH TO INNOVATION

ALDER
HILL
PRESS

Creatively Ever After:
A Path to Innovation

by Alicia Arnold

Alder Hill books may be purchased for educational, business, or sales promotional use. For information please write: Special Markets Department, Alder Hill Press, P.O. Box 563, Hanover, MA 02339

To book the author for speaking engagements, seminars, or training please visit http://alicia-arnold.com

Cataloging-in-Publication Data

    Arnold, Alicia.
        Creatively ever after : a path to innovation / Alicia
    Arnold.
        p. cm.
        Includes bibliographical references and index.
        ISBN: 978-0-9834405-1-2

        1. Creative ability in business. 2. Problem solving.
    I. Title.

    HD53.A76 2011   658.4'094
                       QBI11-200020

Cover and Interior Layout by T.L. Price Freelance
Illustrated by Mike Swaim

For Garrett and Bradley

Contents

ACKNOWLEDGMENTS

Writing *Creatively Ever After* has been a journey. Every day of the past four years has been a learning experience. During these times I was most grateful for the countless individuals who provided encouragement, inspiration and guidance. A special thank you to:

Patty Pfitsch, who helped me find
my voice as an author.

Blair Miller, who planted the seed for this book.

Bea Parnes, Sid Parnes, Sue Keller-Mathers, Marci
Segal, Tara Bissett, Paul Reali, my brother Bill Ng,
and my husband, John Arnold for providing early
feedback which shaped the storyline and direction.

My brother Michael Ng, my sister Jennifer
Dolan and my mother Virginia Ng,
who shared their positive energy.

Gregg Fraley, Whitney Ferre and Tim Hurson, who took the time to share lessons on the business of writing.

My fellow creativity colleagues, friends, and social network – your camaraderie, tweets, and words of wisdom motivated me to keep writing.

WELCOME

Welcome to the creative community! This book is the result of my decades in the business world toiling to bring creative concepts, solutions, and approaches to life. Throughout my career in advertising and marketing, I wondered why creativity was so difficult. I wondered about the many starts and stops during creative projects, the many changes in direction, and why so many good ideas ended up on the cutting room floor. Years later, I earned a Master of Science in Creative Studies and joined the ranks of creativity scholars. In *Creatively Ever After*, I share my learning on how adopting a creative process can make "big-C" (transformational creativity) and "little-c" (everyday creativity) efforts more attainable, more effective, and more efficient.

In a *Bloomberg Businessweek* article entitled "Building a Creative Organization," I wrote about a holistic model for organizations to deliberately increase creativity—the four

Ps of creativity. While it takes all four Ps—People, Process, Product, and Press—to bring what exists in our imaginations to life, *Creatively Ever After* provides a detailed look into the realm of creative process. While I was writing this book, two questions arose. First, what creative process should I base the book upon? Second, what format should I use for the book?

What creative process?

In answering this question, I felt it was important to use a tried-and-tested method. There are many methods of teaching creativity. However, none is as globally accepted, well-tested, and scientifically valid as the Osborn-Parnes Creative Problem Solving Process (CPS).

CPS is a structured method for generating novel and useful solutions to problems. It has been widely researched and proven to be both valid and reliable in building creative thinking skills. CPS was developed by Alex Osborn and Sidney Parnes in the 1950s and has been tested worldwide over the decades. Through testing, CPS was proven effective with adults and school children within academia, the workplace, for-profit, not-for-profit, and many other settings. The steps in the CPS process were modeled to match the way a person's mind naturally works and can be used as a whole or in parts.

In history, there are many examples of creative endeavors where individuals relied on creativity to bring what existed in their imaginations to life. Since about 400 B.C., humans tried many ways to fly like birds. Leonardo da Vinci was one of the first to document real studies of flight. In 1480 A.D., da Vinci recorded hundreds of illustrated theories of flight and even designed plans for an Ornithopter flying machine. Hundreds of years and many advances later, hot air balloons and gliders paved the way for Wilbur and Oliver Wright's first flight. In examining the Wright brothers' attempts to fly, we discover that their endeavors map to the CPS process:

☀ **Identify the Goal, Wish, or Challenge** – Wilbur and Oliver dreamed of flying. They were obsessive in their quest and shared their dream with the world. By verbalizing their Goal, Wish, or Challenge, the Wright brothers set the stage to solve one of the greatest challenges in history.

☀ **Gather Data** – Wilbur and Oliver were deliberate in their quest to fly. They spent many years studying and learning all they could about the early attempts at flight. The two even wrote letters to the Smithsonian requesting information about flight experiments.

☀ **Clarify the Problem** – The Wright brothers identified all the problems that would need to be solved in order to fly.

These problems included how the wind affected flight, how different-shaped machines flew, how to control flight, and many more.

☀ **Generate Ideas** – Wilbur and Oliver developed many different ideas on how to solve the problems they had identified. For example, they used wing warping, or a method for arching the wingtips, to control the aircraft's motion and balance. The two tinkered with many ideas and failed experiments in order to overcome all the roadblocks they faced.

☀ **Develop the Solution** – Bringing together the best of their ideas, the Wright brothers built and tested a full-size glider. Based on this first manned flight, Wilbur and Oliver refined their solution and built an even bigger glider. Over the next four years, the Wrights tested and refined further.

☀ **Plan for Action** – In 1903, knowing they were on to something, the Wright brothers requested a patent application to protect their invention, thus paving the way for a business in aviation. Shortly thereafter Wilbur Wright completed the first successful manned flight.

What format for the book?

With a creative process in hand, the next question became the format. To me, there is nothing worse than reading pages of dry text meant to impart an important lesson, only to have the useful concept overshadowed by technical explanations and complex terminology. I believe that learning should be an adventure, a simple, memorable experience that engages the senses, entertains, and teaches valuable skills while providing immediately useful tools and techniques.

Given the complexity of creativity, I struggled with presenting the dryness of fact. That's when I recalled the energy and childlike wonder that existed when using nursery rhymes to teach creativity. In my teaching of CPS with companies of all sizes, nursery rhymes helped clients tap into their sense of playfulness, opened their minds to creativity, and allowed leaders to bring new thinking to their toughest business challenges. Even top executives let down their guard and let creativity flow. This gave life to the fable format.

The fable provided a framework to bridge the gap between the dryness of fact and the pleasure of fiction. By using the familiar "Jack and Jill" nursery rhyme, I set out to employ CPS to demonstrate how new ways of thinking could help Jack and Jill solve a problem many have taken for granted as unchangeable—that of tumbling down the hill. As I wrote, I married the fictional description, action, and dialogue in the Jack and Jill story with the nonfiction CPS process, sidebar material, and real-life examples to create a modern tale.

As you read and practice the creativity techniques from this book, I encourage you to apply CPS to your challenges and to share your learning with your co-workers, family, and friends. Creativity is a valuable gift that lasts a lifetime.

To learn more visit http//alicia-arnold.com

or http://twitter.com/alicarnold

I wish you all the best in your creative endeavors!

FOREWORD

In the early 1990s, I was looking for people who shared my interest in unlocking the mysteries of creative thinking. I was a member of one of the leading online service providers at the time, Compuserve, and scoured its chat forums for people I might connect with. Among the hundreds of these threaded discussion groups was one, simply called, the Creativity Forum, run by a man named Peter Lloyd.

The Creativity Forum was an eye-opener for me. It was populated by people from all over the world, many of whom are now well-known creativity theorists, practitioners, and advocates — Roger von Oech, Joyce Wycoff, and Gregg Fraley, among them. These people, and many others, participated in stimulating, lively, and sometimes flaming exchanges about the nature of creativity, its importance, why it seemed to be more prevalent in some domains than others, techniques for enhancing it, and many others.

One of the questions that surfaced was whether or not creativity could be taught. Two strong camps quickly emerged: those who held that creativity was innate — either you were lucky enough to have been born with it, or not — and those who thought creativity was a skill that could be learned and developed. Our discussion was a subset of the larger nature/nurture controversy that has occupied mind-scientists and philosophers for over a century.

I was on the side of creativity as a learnable skill. I knew from personal experience that I was able to enhance my own creative thinking using simple tools I had stumbled upon. Often, when I got stuck on a writing assignment, I noticed I would stare blankly at my bookshelves. I would catch the names and authors of the books, as well as, splashes of color and partial cover images. These seemingly random words and images, having nothing directly to do with what I was working on, often stimulated me to see a new and productive angle on my problem. My mind would begin to make connections between these disparate inputs and the work I was doing. Thoughts would stream, collide, and churn until, quite suddenly and unexpectedly, I was able to see a breakthrough.

If this simple technique could help me be more creative, surely it could help others. Surely others had discovered it. Surely it could be taught – and practiced, and refined.

Most people recognize that coaching and practice helps athletes improve performance. Of course, some people are blessed with more athletic potential than others, but regardless of their starting point, or their ultimate capacity, it's clear that in the physical realm, just about anyone can improve. Tennis players can learn productive ways to grip their rackets. Golfers can improve the mechanics of their swing. Runners can adopt more efficient motions. And, in all these cases, efficiency, precision, and endurance could be enhanced through training.

If people could learn to use their bodies better, why not their minds?

Other Creativity Forum contributors had different points of view. Of course, we were never able to resolve our nature/nurture arguments. Despite hurling our opinions at one another, our evidence was anecdotal and not scientific. Convinced of my position, but frustrated I couldn't defend it effectively; I decided to do some research.

In terms of theory, my initial literature reviews were inconclusive. The scientific community seemed as divided on the issue as our lay group, with as many papers supporting nature as nurture — and a few acknowledging the importance of both.

In terms of practice, however, the picture that emerged was far from inconclusive.

Over the years I've conducted thousands of informal interviews with people about what I call *shower thinking*, that free-flow of thought that many experience while standing under a stream of warm water. Of course, not everyone *shower thinks* in the shower. Many report doing it in bed just as they drift off to sleep, or shortly after they wake. Many do it when driving or riding in a car – others while biking, running, during meditation, or during repetitive tasks such as washing the dishes. But, regardless of location or circumstance, *shower thinking* seems to be a near-universal phenomenon.

Though everyone seems to do it, *shower thinking* has some obvious practical limitations – the main one being people usually forget most of the ideas that flit through their minds by the time they towel off. But, might there be a way to encourage this free-flow of ideas in other settings? Might people be able to harness *shower thinking* and apply it more effectively to solving problems and inventing the new? And if so, what might that produce?

My searches eventually led me to a discipline called creative problem solving. This method for training and facilitating more productive approaches to creativity, discovery, and invention was developed by advertising exec, Alex Osborn and Dr. Sid Parnes of Buffalo State University.

In 1941, at the height of his Madison Avenue career, Osborn noticed that some creative meetings were far more productive than others. He discovered that these meetings tended to have the following characteristics:

1) All ideas were entertained. Judgment of ideas was reserved for later.

2) Wild ideas were welcome.

3) A large number of ideas were encouraged.

4) People were encouraged to build on their own ideas and those of others.

These four simple guidelines became the basis for a technique Osborn first called *Thinking Up* (his colleagues later popularized the term *Brainstorming*, which stuck). Though not practiced deliberately, these same basic principles are exactly what we do when we *shower think*. We leap from idea to idea, making all sorts of fantastical connections, without worrying whether our ideas are either wise or wacky, and we do it as long as we're in the shower, with so many ideas tumbling out we can barely remember them once we've dried off.

The advantages of Osborn's *Brainstorming* was that it multiplied the thinking resource by the number of people in the room, and it offered the possibility of recording and collecting the ideas generated for later use.

What Osborn had demonstrated was that people were able to learn a simple set of behaviors that could increase their output both in terms of quantity and quality. In other words, they really could learn to be more creative and to think better.

Some years later, Osborn teamed up with a young psychology professor, named Dr. Sid Parnes, and began combining *brainstorming* guidelines with a five-step (later six-step) process for generating and evaluating useful ideas in virtually any domain. It became known as Osborn-Parnes Creative Problem Solving process, or CPS.

Since then, thousands and thousands of people have learned this simple, yet powerful system of thinking more productively, more effectively, more creatively. CPS, in turn, has spun off a large number of variants as other thinkers continue to refine and develop the process.

Foreword

In this book, Alicia Arnold takes you through CPS, step-by-step, with a lively, entertaining approach that is both easy to read and easy to apply. I encourage you to read it not just once, but several times to begin to see the beauty and subtlety of the Osborn-Parnes Creative Problem Solving framework. You will discover, as have thousands of others, that you really can learn and develop your creative thinking capacity. By honing your thinking skills, you are guaranteed to have more ideas, better ideas, more often.

Consider yourself lucky. You are about to embark on a remarkable journey.

Tim Hurson
Author of *Think Better*

CHAPTER ONE

The Way It Was

JACK AND JILL WENT UP THE HILL
TO FETCH A PAIL OF WATER
JACK FELL DOWN AND BROKE HIS CROWN
AND JILL CAME TUMBLING AFTER

Jack took a deep, cleansing breath and inhaled the smell of the rich dirt, earthy moss, and fresh morning dew. The crispness of the night rain lingered in the air. For a passing moment, Jack allowed the rhythmic sound of birds greeting the day to overtake the negative chatter brewing in his mind. Soon enough, the snapping of twigs beneath his footsteps and the dampness of leaves against his skin broke his woodland trance.

Jack's senses sharpened and his relaxed state gave way to anxiety as he thought about the challenge that lay ahead of him. Making his way up the vertical incline, Jack swore that today would be the day he conquered the hill. He raised his fist in the air and defiantly shouted, "You're not going to get the best of me. Not today!"

Jack thought, "Just because I tumble down the hill every day doesn't mean I am going to do so today." As he spoke, he could feel his muscles tightening. He knew if he didn't ease the tension, he would fold under the pressure. To prepare himself mentally for the challenge of conquering the hill, Jack used a focusing technique he had learned at karate.

He started by focusing all his concentration into one attentive stream. In his mind's eye, Jack vividly pictured the triumphant moment. With his eyes closed tightly and his ears blocked to filter out the extraneous noise, Jack quieted the negative chatter in his mind. As he pictured what success would look like, the knot began to unravel in his shoulder and the tension flowed from Jack's body. He continued the visualization by picturing the arch of his foot contouring to the shape of a small stone as he marched up the craggy hill. Jack envisioned his arm extending as he reached for the pail of water. Next, he felt a gratifying smile spread across his face as he confidently chose a less treacherous path. Sparks of joy radiated throughout Jack's body as his legs moved instinctively across the terrain. In Jack's imagination he succeeded in conquering the hill. At that very moment, Jack pictured himself standing triumphantly at the base of the hill holding a full bucket of water—no slipping, no tripping, and certainly no tumbling.

By using the powers of positive thinking to picture what a successful descent down the hill would feel like, Jack was able to turn his stress into a swell of excitement. He had been preparing for this challenge his entire life. Each and every day for as long as Jack could remember, he had tried to conquer the hill. At this point, he was sure he had tried at least a hundred different paths down the hill. Yesterday, Jack almost perfected the trip. In fact, he didn't slip until the very end of the path and lost only a small amount of the water.

However, as tenacious as Jack was in trying the different paths, his patience was wearing thin. His eighteenth birthday was quickly approaching and he wanted to achieve his goal before the milestone day. Jack had to hurry. His birthday was just a mere week away. "That should be enough time," thought Jack. If he didn't succeed by his eighteenth birthday, Jack planned to give up hope of conquering the hill. After all, how many failures could a guy endure? The importance Jack placed on the day made him feel nauseated. Was it fear causing his queasiness or was it just hunger?

As Jack opened his eyes and slowly returned to the sights and sounds of the forest, he recognized the familiar pattern of Jill's shirt. He knew she had been studying him. As if reading Jack's mind, Jill said, "Jack, don't you understand? The definition of insanity is doing the same thing over and over again and expecting a different result. Do you really think you're going to find a better path down the hill today? What makes this day any different from the last hundred days—or the last seventeen years, for that matter?"

Jack resisted taking Jill's bait. He felt a war of words beginning to brew, but he knew that quarreling with Jill would only distract him from the cause. As much as Jack was a dreamer and quick to action, Jill was rooted in reality. In Jack's point of view, Jill didn't have an original bone in her body. She never had any ideas of her own and always squelched his suggestions. It seemed that all Jill was good for was asking questions. Questions, questions, questions—all day and all night!

For Jack, being a twin was difficult. Popular belief held that twins were alike, but Jack didn't feel Jill was like him at all. What perplexed him most was how dissimilar they were when it came to how they approached the world. Jack was fearless; Jill was cautious. Jack liked to challenge the rules; Jill liked to live within the rules. Jack relished change; Jill enjoyed the status quo. It wasn't that Jack didn't love his sister. They were just different. However, spying Jill, Jack began to smile.

For, at the end of the day, regardless of all their differences, the twins were inseparable.

Continuing to taunt Jack, Jill yelled, "Hey, bro! What's your hare-brained scheme this time? You really need to get a grip on reality. Don't you realize that falling down the hill is our destiny?"

Jack's smile faded. He gritted his teeth against Jill's sarcasm. Rolling his eyes with disgust, Jack replied, "Jill, maybe for once you could help me figure out a way to solve the problem, rather than getting in my way. You should give it a try sometime! If you worked *with* me rather than *against* me, we might make significant progress."

Jack's temper flared. He began to see red. But he knew instinctively not to push the issue. He could feel the tears welling up in Jill's eyes even before he saw them. Jack whispered under his breath, "You might be great at dishing out grief, but you never could take it." He knew just when to stop pushing Jill. This was one of those moments. Jack cooled his temper and let Jill's comments pass. He motioned for her to go forward and the two continued up the hill in silence.

At the top of the hill, Jack threw the pail into the well. Once it was filled with water, he tugged on the crank and slowly hoisted the pail back up. Carefully, Jack worked the pail off the hook and began to share with Jill his new idea for how to get down the hill. He spoke with a calm and determined voice. "Yesterday, we tried the path to the right and nearly made it all the way down the hill. Today," he said, pointing, "we're going to take the same path until the bend, then change course and walk across the briar patch. It'll be a bit longer and we'll have to walk through some thorns, but the ground is more level, so we should be able to steady our footing."

Jack braced himself for Jill's reply, but all he heard were the birds chirping. He glanced up and caught the look of dismay in Jill's eye. He thought she would protest, but surprisingly, Jill lined up behind Jack and signaled him to lead the way. Perhaps Jill's stomach was rumbling and she knew the quickest way to get to breakfast was to follow Jack down the path.

Jack quickened his step and led the way. He was nearing the briar patch when a small stone caused him to misstep. Jack nimbly rebalanced his weight. He let out a screech but maintained his grip on the pail. Luckily, Jack was able to land solidly on two feet. With a sheepish grin, he admitted to Jill, "Boy! That was close! We're almost to the bottom. Just a few more steps through the thorns and we'll be golden," he encouraged her.

Jack's adrenaline rush had just subsided when a thick, gnarly vine caught his shoelace. Hopping unsteadily on one foot while balancing the pail, Jack tried mightily to tug his shoelace free. In the end, it was no use. "Wahhhh!" he screamed as he lurched forward and fell, face-first, into a patch of prickly thorns. Like clockwork, Jill lost her footing and tumbled along behind him.

Defeated, Jack swallowed his disappointment. Warily, he extended a sore arm and lifted his hand, brushing across a walnut-sized welt forming on his forehead. Painstakingly, Jack looked up at Jill and sighed. "I just don't know why we can't find a better way to fetch the water. We've tumbled down this hill all our lives. By the time we get to the bottom, we've lost all the water. We never have enough water for the day, which means more trips to the well and more bumps and bruises. I can't take it anymore. I despise this hill!"

Brushing dirt off her pants, Jill turned her attention to her scraped knee. Then in a quiet voice she whispered, "Jack, we've tried hundreds of ways down the hill and none have worked. No matter what we do, we just keep falling. What makes you think we can change our story? We live in the Land of Nursery Rhyme, after all. Things just don't change in Nursery Rhyme. Give it up!"

Chapter 1: Questions to Consider

As you read this book and apply the techniques to your unique situation, ask yourself:

☀ In what ways is Jack creative?

☀ In what ways is Jill creative?

☀ Peer pressure often dampens creativity. In what ways did Jill squelch Jack's creativity?

☀ In what ways are you creative?

☀ How might you apply the techniques learned in this book to your situation?

☀ What have you read that resonates? Why?

☀ Is there anything that surprises you? Why?

☀ What strategies can you use to unlock your creativity?

☀ Time pressure is also a detractor to creativity. How did time pressure work against Jack's creativity?

☀ How are time pressure and peer pressure detractors to your creativity?

Chapter 1: Setting the Tone for Creativity

Setting the tone for creativity begins with a prepared mind. A prepared mind allows imagination to flourish and invites creative thinking. One of the best ways to evoke creativity is to relax, or, in other words, de-stress. When it comes to stress, it may seem as if many situations bring about demands that require you to stretch beyond your comfort zone. The key to overcoming stress is to recognize that *you* are in control of how you respond.

Time pressure and peer pressure are two things that squelch creativity. Nothing dampens creativity more than putting a time limit on the imagination and exploration process. What about peer pressure? Peer pressure manifests itself in verbal and nonverbal ways. Both are equally damaging. When it comes to being creative, people often roll their eyes in a "that idea will never work!" manner. This is just as destructive as someone actually saying, "Your idea will never work." Ideas are like tall blades of grass. Great ideas stand head and shoulders above the rest. But

Continued on 12

Continued from 11

watch out! The taller the blades of grass, the more apt they are to get mowed down.

When it comes to relaxing, telling someone to "relax" can be much easier than the act of relaxation itself. Stress tends to breed negativity. In order to reduce stress, you need to regain a positive mindset. Engage in activities that make you feel good like dancing, listening to music, practicing yoga, swimming, or walking to bring about positive emotions and reduce stress. But, remember to practice moderation. Too much of anything can be unhealthy.

Grab a pen and make a list of stress-reducing activities that work for you. What have you done in the past to relax and de-stress? The next time you find yourself in a stressful situation, refer to your list and set a positive tone by engaging in a stress-busting activity. This will help unlock your creative energies.

Light Bulb Moment

Jack thought carefully about Jill's comment about things never changing in Nursery Rhyme. In considering all the possibilities for paths down the hill, Jack had an "aha!" moment. It was as if a light bulb had gone on. He replied, "Jill, what you said about things not changing may have some truth. But if we look beyond Nursery Rhyme, things do change. In the Land of People, things have changed a great deal over time. It used to take years for humans to travel the world by ship. Nowadays, people circle the globe by air and it takes no time at all. Perhaps we can take a cue from them. People have the ability to change their situations and create their own destinies. We should be able to do the same."

Jill stood up, crossed her arms, and said crossly, "Jack, you are impossible! Don't you understand this *is* our destiny? We are not people. We live in Nursery Rhyme. We go up the hill, you fall down the hill, and I come tumbling after. It is just the way things are—the way things have been since the beginning of time. After all these years, you should be used to it by now."

Jack was at his wits' end. He did all he could to shut out Jill's comments. By ignoring Jill, he was able to clear a pathway for new thinking. Jack felt he was onto something when he discovered how people invented the airplane to change their destinies. He knew a solution was close. All he had to do was concentrate a bit harder. Jack thought, "If only Jill would stop pressuring me to give up my dreams, I might be able to figure out a solution!"

Jack pleaded, "Jill, just because things are the way they always have been doesn't mean they can't change. Wouldn't it be great if we could fetch the water without hurting ourselves? Just think! Rather than nursing our bruises and wearing ourselves out by fetching the water, we could spend our days dancing to Old King Cole's fiddle music." Jack recited,

"OLD KING COLE WAS A MERRY OLD SOUL
AND A MERRY OLD SOUL WAS HE.
HE CALLED FOR HIS PIPE, AND HE
CALLED FOR HIS BOWL,
AND HE CALLED FOR HIS FIDDLERS THREE..."

Jack continued, "Just think! Mom wouldn't have to spend all her free time cooped up in the house mending our ripped clothes. This problem is bigger than just the two of us. It is consuming our entire family."

Breaking Jack's productive energy, Jill retorted, "Didn't you hear me? What makes you think *we* are capable of changing our story when *we* haven't been able to do so in the past? How many more times do we need to try? I'm tired of following all your silly new paths down the hill. No matter what we do, we still fail. Give it up!"

Frustrated, Jack kept turning over Jill's response in his mind. As he thought about what Jill had said, he formed a mental picture of the phrase "change our story." The phrase grew larger and larger until it consumed his thoughts. At that moment, another connection popped into his head. In his mind's eye, Jack pictured the phrases "Old King Cole" and "change our story!" going round and round like wooden horses on a carousel.

A wide grin formed on Jack's face. His eyes lit up. He turned to Jill and said, "I have it! Old King Cole knows something we don't. Old King Cole did not always have a happy ending. His story was just as bleak as ours—as bleak as many others in Nursery Rhyme. But something changed. Let's talk to Old King Cole and figure out what he did to change his story."

Jill rolled her eyes and opened her mouth to criticize, but Jack interrupted. He could clearly see Jill didn't remember the way it was with Old King Cole. Jack chanted a version of the Old King Cole story that existed within the memories of just a select few in Nursery Rhyme. He recited,

"Old King Cole was a grumpy old soul,

and a grumpy old soul was he.

He barked for pipe,

and he whined for his bowl,

and he yelled for his fiddlers three..."

To Jack, it seemed like a million years ago when Old King Cole was grumpy. The picture of the grumpy king was a distant, faded memory that would have been forgotten if he hadn't been so driven to continue coming up with ideas, or if Jill hadn't triggered the connection of looking to see how others had changed their stories.

Jack watched Jill intently and noticed the change in her facial expression as she remembered the king—first as a grumpy old soul, then as a happy old soul. Jill softened her stance and leaned forward. It was as if a great weight had been lifted from her shoulders. Jack asked, "Jill, what's on your mind?"

Jill answered, "We've tried so many different ways of getting down the hill. I couldn't bear to fail yet again. I was convinced things didn't change in Nursery Rhyme until you reminded me of how people changed their destinies and, more importantly, of how Old King Cole used to be grumpy. The king's story has been a happy one for so long that I had almost forgotten it was not always that way. Maybe change does happen in Nursery Rhyme! Maybe we do have the power to change our story."

"Yeah, that's right, sis," said Jack smugly. "I told you that you should listen to me rather than fighting me all the time. You should just do what I say. We'd save a lot of time and aggravation. Enough chit-chatting! Let's find Old King Cole and figure out how to change our story."

Jill responded, "Yeah, let's go before your head gets too big for your own good. Remember all of those unsuccessful ideas for traversing the hill? Those were yours too. Just because you might be on to something this time doesn't mean you're right all the time."

Chapter 2: Association of Ideas

Alex Osborn, known widely as the person who popularized the term *brainstorming*, believed that ideas led to other ideas. Osborn called this phenomenon *associationism* or *reintegration*. According to Osborn, association works better for those who are driven to imagination and whose minds are better stocked.

Jack is an "idea person"; thus, he was able to associate people being able to change their destiny and King Cole's ability to change his story as a way to help solve his problem. Throughout history, there are many examples of associationism in people's daily lives.

For instance, in 1964, when the first Japanese Bullet Train was developed, it was able to travel at speeds of 120 miles an hour. Unfortunately, when a train going that fast exited the tunnel, it created a loud boom. In examining the problem, engineer and bird enthusiast Eiji Nakatsu looked to nature for a solution. He realized that the train was pushing air in front of it, forming a wall of wind. When

Continued on 21

Continued from 20

this wall collided with the air outside the tunnel, it created a loud sound. Nakatsu studied diver birds, known as kingfishers. These birds were able to plunge into the water from far distances to catch fish without making a ripple. Piggybacking on this insight, Nakatsu designed the front of the train almost identical to the kingfisher's bill.

The science behind copying Mother Nature to solve challenges is called biomimicry. Today, biomimetics is a rapidly growing industry that has provided ideas for solving a host of challenges.

In thinking about your challenge, ask yourself:

- What associations come to mind when you think of your problem?

- What might be all the ways to leverage nature to help solve the problem?

Capture your thoughts in words or in pictures. Feel free to sketch the associations that come to mind. As you think of other associations, add them to your list. Refer back to this exercise as you work through your problem. Sometimes associations can help in surprising ways.

CHAPTER THREE

A Visit with
Old King Cole

Jack and Jill rushed over to Old King Cole's castle to ask him how he had changed the ending of his story. There they found the king dancing jovially to fiddler's music. He was accompanied by the cat, cow, dog, dish, and spoon from "Hey Diddle Diddle." Jack studied the king as he step-danced regally toward platters of food. He smiled to himself as King Cole popped a handful of grapes into his mouth.

Taking in the blissful scene, Jack whispered to Jill, "'Hey Diddle Diddle' is a happy story, as well." He straightened his back, lifted his chin, and recited,

"HEY DIDDLE DIDDLE.

THE CAT AND THE FIDDLE.

THE COW JUMPED OVER THE MOON.

THE LITTLE DOG LAUGHED TO SEE SUCH SPORT,

AND THE DISH RAN AWAY WITH THE SPOON."

Jack continued, "They must all know something we don't. I'm guessing the king's guests changed the endings of their stories too. I have a great feeling about this day. I am convinced that we might still have a shot at conquering the hill before our eighteenth birthday."

When the music came to a stop, Jack waved to the king. Old King Cole walked over and gave Jack a great big pat on the back. "My friend, how great to see you! I can't help but notice you look a bit distraught. What can I do to help?" asked the king.

Jack took King Cole up on his invitation to discuss his challenge. He and Jill took a seat next to King Cole. Jack described the pair's predicament while Jill provided support and encouragement. Jack told King Cole it was of "utmost" importance to conquer the hill within the week. Taking a deep breath, Jack walked the king through the many alternatives they had tried, including yesterday's near success.

As Jack shared the story, his shoulders slumped and his voice became quieter. The more he spoke, the more deflated he became. Although Jack didn't like to admit defeat, he knew this problem was a tough one. In fact, he admitted to the king, "I'm starting to doubt whether the problem is even solvable."

The king replied, "Jack and Jill, I believe the two of you are well on your way to solving your problem. I say this because sharing your situation with me and asking for help tells me you acknowledge your challenge and are open to a new perspective. Sometimes all a stubborn problem needs is a bit of new thinking. If your mind is open to new points of view, you are indeed a step closer to finding a solution." The king continued, "You know, I was once in a seemingly impossible predicament like yours. I suspect that is why you are here. You are quite possibly one of the few citizens of Nursery Rhyme who remembered I was not always so happy."

Closing his eyes and taking a deep breath, the king quietly admitted, "I used to be so miserable that my closest friends and family went to extremes to avoid me. Regardless of all my possessions, I always felt lonely."

Jack leaned forward in his seat and whispered, wide-eyed, "What did you do? How did you change your story?"

"After a great deal of searching for answers," the king replied, "I met a delightful woman named Greta. I shared my situation with her. After hearing my story, she eagerly introduced me to something called the Osborn-Parnes Creative Problem Solving Process, or, as I like to call it, CPS. Now, when I have a problem I am stuck on—one that makes me stressed or keeps me up at night—I turn to CPS. It's a simple, repeatable way to bring new thinking to my challenges."

"Did I hear you right," asked Jack? "Gretel is the one who helped you?"

"Actually," King Cole replied, "While their names are similar, Greta and Gretel are two different people. Greta is the one who is trained in creative problem solving.

King Cole grabbed a notebook and a pencil. He sketched the CPS process while Jack watched. The king continued, "CPS consists of six steps that you can use as a whole or in parts. You can start with the first step and go all the way through, or you can use the steps in a non-linear order—it depends on your challenge."

Here's what the CPS process looks like when used as a whole:

- Identify the Goal, Wish, or Challenge

- Gather Data

- Clarify the Problem

- Generate Ideas

- Develop Solutions

- Plan for Action

The king looked up from his notebook. "If the two of you join me for breakfast, we can continue our conversation. I always think better with a full stomach."

Jack realized he was starving and only then noticed a delectably sweet smell wafting through the air. He and Jill enthusiastically accepted King Cole's invitation. Over perfectly cooked chocolate chip pancakes, King Cole continued to share how distraught he had been about being grumpy. Although he had tried many ways to change the ending of his story, nothing seemed to work. The king admitted that he even tried to make up for his sadness by using his great wealth to throw lavish banquets. "However," he shared, "deep down, I was truly unhappy."

Gripping the edge of his seat, Jack noted, "But it seems you were able to solve your problem. CPS must be really fantastic. Can you show us how it works?"

King Cole answered, "I believe you would benefit from having an expert guide you. Why don't you head over to Greta's? I will give her a call to let her know you are on your way. She is always happy to help." King Cole reached for a map and marked the route to Greta's cottage. Then he added, "If you trust the CPS process, you will find a solution to your challenge."

"Trust?" asked Jack skeptically.

"Think of learning CPS as an investment in you," replied King Cole. "Although your immediate challenge is conquering the hill, the hill is a metaphor for any number of tough challenges you might be looking to solve. CPS is good for both "big-C" creativity, which we also call transformational creativity, and "little-c" creativity, which is your everyday creativity. The difference lies in how far you stretch your thinking."

Jack replied, "I'm sold. After all these years, if all it takes is a little trust, I guess I'm willing to give it a try." He reached for the map.

But before Jack could take possession, Jill stopped him and addressed the king "Before we go to Greta's, I need to ask one question, King Cole. What did you find most useful about working with Greta?"

Jack scoffed, "Aww, Jill, we have what we're looking for. We know the king used CPS to solve his problem. Stop slowing us down with your silly questions. How is learning what the king found most useful relevant to our situation?" he demanded to know.

Jill retorted, "By figuring out what worked for the king, we can piggyback on his learning to help us get to a solution more quickly."

"Hmm," Jack said thoughtfully, "so what you're saying is that we should take it slower now in order to move more quickly later? I don't know if I buy into your logic. But let's just cut to the chase. King, what did you find most valuable?"

Placing his chin on the palms of his hands, the King pondered the question and answered carefully, "I have to admit, I've never given it much thought until now. But I guess, at the end of the day, what I found most valuable in working with Greta was her guidance in helping me clarify my problem."

"What does that mean?" asked Jack.

"Well," King Cole continued, "before working with Greta, I blamed everyone except myself for my misfortune. Greta helped me realize that I could use CPS to address problems only where I had ownership, motivation, and the need for imagination. In other words, I needed to have responsibility for the problems, I needed to want to solve them, and I needed to use creative thinking to come to a solution. She also helped me create problem statements using open-ended questions. I went through these problem statements one by one and checked them for ownership, motivation, and the need for imagination. To my surprise, I realized I had wasted a lot of time over the years solving problems that were not mine to solve. And, soon enough, I came to the conclusion it was not anyone else or anything else, but *me* who was at the root of my challenges. This helped me see that my feelings followed the actions I took. And this, my friend, was just the catalyst I needed to get past my limited view of the situation and take control of my actions to change my story." Taking a pause to pull together his thoughts, the king continued, "Phrasing problems using open-ended questions freed my mind to knock down roadblocks and to believe I was truly capable of solving the problems."

Jack considered the king's response while he studied the drawing of the CPS process. He said, "I see how the CPS process can be applied to a wide variety of challenges. Your situation and ours are very different, but what they have in common is that they are both stubborn problems without apparent solutions. I can see how taking the time to define what the actual problem is can help influence the solution."

Jack softened his stance on Jill's question to the king. "I guess this was helpful after all," he admitted.

Jill piped up energetically, "King Cole, you referred to crafting problem statements so that they are formatted as open-ended questions. Jack says I don't have a creative bone in my body, but I'm good at asking questions. Perhaps being skilled at asking questions is creative? I never thought of questions as a way to clarify a problem before, but I can now see how each question can help hone a direction—like making your way out of a fog."

"But," Jack snickered, "there's a difference between your questions and open-ended questions. If you remember from school, open-ended questions are exploratory. They are questions you cannot answer with a simple yes or no." Jack searched his memory for an example and continued, "When you asked if I thought I would really find a better path down the hill today—that was a close-ended question. However, if you rephrased the question as, 'What might be all the ways to find a better way down the hill?' that would be an open-ended question. Answering the second question requires more than just a simple yes or no. "

"Precisely," quipped King Cole. "You kids really caught on quickly. Jack, you should continue thinking up new ideas and testing them out. And Jill, be sure to make the most of your gift of questioning by asking open-ended questions. You are both on a solid track. Tap into your talents."

Jack blushed at the king's compliment. Even though King Cole was friends with his family, kudos from his majesty was still a big deal. With a burst of newfound energy and wasting little time, Jack and Jill took turns shaking hands with King Cole and enthusiastically thanking him for his time and for sharing his story. Waving a heartfelt goodbye to the king, Jack gave Jill a nudge and the two scurried off to find Greta.

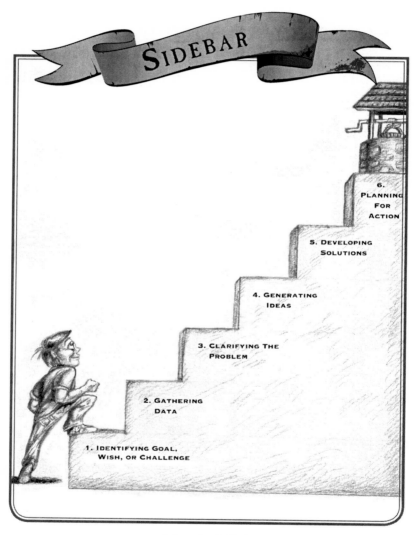

Visual of CPS

Map of Greta's cottage

Goals, Wishes,
and Challenges

Jack reached into his pocket to touch the map and make sure it was still there. A part of him felt like the day's adventure had all been just a dream. After seventeen years, how could it be that a random argument with Jill would lead the twins to King Cole? Perhaps it wasn't so random after all. Maybe because conquering the hill was planted in his mind when the opportunity to speak with the king presented itself, Jack was ready to seize the moment. Jack held the thick, scratchy parchment paper, comforted by the roughness of its touch. "Yes, this day is real," he said.

Spotting a bright array of fragrant wildflowers, Jack knew they were nearing Greta's. In the distance, the walkway to Greta's cottage was a welcoming sight. As Jack and Jill made their way down the winding path, hummingbirds darted back and forth, drinking the sweet nectar from the long-necked flowers. Jack caught Jill's eye and said, "What an enchanting place. I have a good feeling about this. But I still find it amazing that we never heard of Greta or CPS before today."

At the door, Jack peeked inside and spied a kindly woman singing as she pulled a tray of brownies out of the oven. Spurred on by both his sweet tooth and his quest, Jack knocked excitedly on the door.

The woman walked to the door and welcomed the guests. "Hello," she sang, shaking their hands. "I am Greta. King Cole called and told me you were on your way." She ushered Jack and Jill into her living room.

As Jack and Jill walked into the sun-filled home and settled into the overstuffed seats, Greta explained that she had worked with many friends in Nursery Rhyme to help them change the endings of their stories. She said, "I learned CPS from people many, many years ago. Not only did I help Old King Cole, but I helped change the endings for "Hey Diddle Diddle" and "Row, Row, Row Your Boat," as well."

Jack smiled. He had guessed correctly about "Hey Diddle Diddle." "And,"commented Jack aloud, "who would have thought "Row, Row, Row Your Boat" was ever an unhappy story?" He melodically recited,

"ROW, ROW, ROW YOUR BOAT
GENTLY DOWN THE STREAM
MERRILY, MERRILY, MERRILY, MERRILY
LIFE IS BUT A DREAM..."

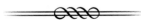

If there was any doubt in his mind before, Jack now knew Greta would help them conquer the hill. After all, if she could help the king and many other friends in Nursery Rhyme, she could surely help the twins. It was only a hill, after all! Right?

After the introduction, Greta invited Jack and Jill to share their story. Both painstakingly provided details of the many ways they had tried to conquer the hill. Unlike the first time he shared the story with King Cole, this time Jack felt greater hope. Sitting with Greta and hearing what she had done for others in Nursery Rhyme reawakened the possibility of conquering the hill. Jack ended the story with an upbeat, "... And that's why we're here!"

Greta thanked Jack and Jill for providing such a vivid account of their efforts. She continued, "The king mentioned that he provided a brief introduction of the CPS process. Now that I've heard your situation, why don't we just dig right in? Let's start with an exercise in wish making."

Greta guided Jack and Jill with ease. She said, "The first step in CPS is identifying your Goal, Wish, or Challenge. With CPS, we use specific language to prepare our minds for the creative journey. You will start each Goal, Wish, or Challenge with the phrase, 'It would be great if...' or 'I wish...'"

She continued, "Goals, Wishes, and Challenges are brief (concise), broad (not detailed or specific) and beneficial (helpful, or good to someone or something) statements of what you would like to accomplish. For example, your wish might be: It would be great if we could stop tumbling down the hill."

Jack exclaimed, "That's exactly our wish. How easy. Now, what's the next step?"

"Not so fast," coached Greta while signaling Jack with her hands to slow down. "You're not going to make just one wish. Between you and Jill, I want you to list as many wishes as you can. Try for at least ten. The more wishes you make, the clearer your goal will become. Coming up with lots of wishes may seem like a stretch, but pushing your mind to go beyond the obvious will help strengthen your solution in the end."

"Okay," replied Jack, "I get it. I suppose this shouldn't be too difficult. We've come this far. We're up for the task."

"That's the winning spirit," encouraged Greta. "Keep up the great work," she cheered. Greta then handed Jack and Jill a set of sticky notes and felt-tip markers. She instructed the pair, "Write one wish per sticky note. Remember to start each wish with the phrase, 'It would be great if…' or 'I wish…' Make sure you write legibly so we can read your wishes afterwards. Once you're done, we will read each sticky note and group similar wishes. Any questions before we start?"

"No questions," chimed Jack. He began writing frantically while Jill took a moment to get going. After a few minutes Jack's pen slowed and Jill's eyes began searching the room.

Jill lamented, "Coming up with wishes is harder than I thought. I'm fresh out of Goals, Wishes, and Challenges. And what happens if my wishes are the same as Jack's?"

Greta smiled a knowing smile and replied, "Quantity begets quality. The more wishes you capture, the better the chances of getting a good one. As for duplicate wishes, they are perfectly acceptable. When we cluster your wishes into similar groups or themes, duplicates will indicate there is interest in that particular area. Now, let's see what we can do about stretching for wishes. Take a close look at your sticky notes. As you do so, I will pose some thought starters. If any of my questions spur a follow-on wish, be sure to capture it. This is called piggybacking on other ideas. Remember to write just one wish per sticky note."

Jack flexed his fingers and concentrated on his sticky notes. Greta began speaking in a relaxed voice and comfortable pace.

Her soothing tone, rhythmic cadence, and guiding questions gave Jack and Jill the fuel to continue wishing. Greta asked,

- What issues are on your mind?

- What do you wish you could change?

- Who has been on your mind? Why?

- What opportunities would you like to take advantage of?

- Imagine yourself one year from today. What are some goals you would like to accomplish?

- What would make you feel happier?

Jack and Jill captured all the wishes that popped into their minds. At the end of wish making, Jack let out a big, deep breath. He rested his pen on the table and yawned. "All of this thinking is making me tired. Concentrating is really hard work."

"It can be," replied Greta. "But I'm sure you'll be happy with the results. Now it's time to read out the wishes. Which of you would like to begin?"

Jack eagerly raised his hand and said, "I'll start... It would be great if we could conquer the hill."

Greta nodded and said, "Jill, do you have anything similar?"

"Yes, I do," Jill said. "I wish we could stop falling down the hill."

Jack added, "It would be great if we needed less water."

The wish making continued and the list grew. As wishes were read, Greta reminded the two to capture any additional wishes that came to mind as a result of hearing the wishes read aloud. The list expanded to include:

☀ It would be great if we could conquer the hill.

☀ I wish we could stop falling down the hill.

☀ It would be great if we had more time for fun.

☀ I wish we could change the ending of our story.

☀ It would be great if we were happy.

☀ I wish we had more energy at the end of the day.

☀ It would be great if we could learn from others.

☀ It would be great to find other ways to get water.

☀ It would be great to stay healthy.

❊ It would be great if we found a safer, more effective way to fetch the water.

"Great job stretching," commented Greta. "You've come a long way in a short time. Any questions before we move on?"

"Yes, I have one question," started Jack. "I set aside a few sticky notes because I wasn't sure if they fit the Goal, Wish, Challenge exercise. The notes say: 'It would be great if I had better shoes. It would be great if we built a public water system. It would be great if Jill and I had protective clothing.' What should I do with these?"

Greta answered, "Great question, Jack. Your instinct was right. Your sticky notes do not belong in the Goal, Wish, or Challenge category. What you've captured in those three notes are ideas masking themselves as Goals, Wishes, and Challenges. Excellent job picking up on that point! Remember earlier when we spoke about accomplishments being broad, brief, and beneficial? What is it that these three sticky notes have in common?"

The answer was waiting at the tip of Jack's tongue. He quickly blurted, "They are the opposite of broad—they are very specific solutions."

Nodding, Greta replied, "You've got it. Now that we've diverged, it is time for us to converge. Diverge, or to practice divergence, means to branch out or seek many possibilities. By stretching for many wishes, we've branched out. To converge, or to practice convergence, means to bring together. Let's examine what we have and see how all these pieces fit together."

Greta rose, picked up Jack's and Jill's notes, and stuck them on her living room wall. She invited Jack and Jill to look over each sticky note carefully to see if there was one that stood head and shoulders above the rest. She described this magical sticky note as "an all-encompassing wish that if accomplished, would help you achieve the other wishes."

Jack and Jill sat on the couch and conferred. Jack said, "I think the last one stands head and shoulders above the rest." He read, "'It would be great if we found a safer, more effective way to fetch the water.' Let's pick that one. It covers the rest of them."

"Hmm," replied Jill. "You might be right, but I need more time to take a closer look. I think there's a pattern forming. Let's group similar sticky notes into categories and see if the last one summarizes the overall wish."

Jack protested, "Come on, Jill! It's so obvious. Let's just choose it and get going."

"J-Jack," Jill stammered, "this won't take long. There aren't that many sticky notes up there. We'll be done in a minute. Just give me some time to think. You're always moving so fast that I never have enough time to process my thoughts." With that, she rose, walked over to the sticky notes, and started moving them into groupings based on theme. "See," she continued, "I'm done. Now let me stand back and take a look. Hmm," she said, pausing, "I guess you're right. I can see how 'It would be great if we found a safer, more effective way to fetch the water' could serve as the higher order wish that would solve the others when we achieve it."

"Nice job converging, Jill!" commented Greta. "I can see you're predisposed to clarifying and developing. The technique you've naturally demonstrated is called Hits and Clustering. You 'hit' or identified all of the sticky notes that were pertinent to the situation. In this case, you deemed them all pertinent, and then you clustered, or grouped, them into themes. Now that you've converged, let's test for ownership, motivation, and need for imagination."

"Fantastic," said Jack, beaming from ear to ear. "It's really easy having you guide us through CPS—really almost as easy as breathing." As Jack resettled himself back into the chair, Greta asked him three questions to clarify whether CPS was a good fit for his challenge.

She began, "Do you have ownership for the challenge? In other words, are you responsible for the situation?"

"What do you mean by that?" asked Jack.

"Well, let's look at an example," replied Greta. "If you see your sister spending her time playing games online with her friends rather than doing her homework and that she is failing her classes as a result, the problem is not yours to solve. It is your sister who is accountable for her actions and for changing her situation. In this example, Jill owns the situation with her failing grades and is the one who needs to fix it. You cannot control another person's actions. The only actions you can control are your own."

"Okay," said Jack. In playing with the explanation of ownership in his mind, Jack saw parallels between the homework example and how he had been trying to change Jill's negative attitude. Jack thought to himself, "Perhaps there is another way—a more productive way—to respond to Jill's sarcasm. I'll have to think about that one later." Switching his attention back to the question of ownership, he answered, "Yes, we do have ownership."

"Now to question number two," continued Greta. "Are you motivated to solve the challenge? In other words, do you really want to take action?"

Jack cheered, "Absolutely!"

"Excellent," said Greta knowingly. "I suspected you would answer 'yes' to that question. So far, you've answered yes to ownership and motivation. I have just one more question to ask you. Does your challenge require imagination?"

Jack paused on the word imagination. Then he told Greta he felt he had a strong imagination and offered all the many paths he had devised down the hill as proof.

Greta replied, "Ah, yes! You do have a great imagination. Being able to come up with as many paths as you have requires great ability to generate ideas. However, you may want to open your mind to other alternatives. New paths may not be the only solution."

"Huh?" questioned Jack guardedly.

"Well, you see," started Greta, "in looking for ideas, you have gone very deep into one area: finding new paths down the hill. But it may be time to dig somewhere else. There may be solutions to your problem that do not involve finding a new path."

"Interesting!" exclaimed Jack. "I guess I hadn't thought of that before. In that case, yes. We do need new thinking to solve our problem."

"Great," said Greta, applauding. She motioned toward the kitchen and offered, "Let's grab a warm brownie and a glass of cold milk before continuing."

"Absolutely!" the twins shouted. The sweet smell of chocolate intensified as they neared the kitchen. Gobbling the brownies and milk, Jack and Jill refueled for the next leg of their journey.

Chapter 4: Goal, Wish or Challenge

Take a moment to practice coming up with Goals, Wishes, and Challenges

Diverge

❋ Generate as many Goals, Wishes, and Challenges as you can using the phrases, "It would be great if..." or "I wish..."

❋ Be sure your Goals, Wishes, and Challenges are phrased positively so that you are working toward achieving something you want, like more free time, and not something you don't, like avoiding hectic days.

❋ Check for ownership, motivation, and the need for imagination.

Converge

❋ End wish making by capturing the one Goal, Wish, or Challenge you will focus on.

Chapter 4: Affective Thinking Tool

Emotions play a big role in creativity. When it comes to solving problems, feeling great about what you're accomplishing helps to increase the energy you have to put toward your endeavor. The feelings you experience tend to follow the actions you take. What this means is, if you want to change the way you feel, you need to change the actions you take. Therefore, it is always a good rule of thumb to test your Goal, Wish, or Challenge against the feelings you want to associate with achieving it.

Below is a list of positive emotions. Feel free to add emotions as you see fit. Put a check mark next to the emotions you would like to feel when you accomplish your Goal, Wish, or Challenge. Now, consider whether you will feel those emotions when you achieve your Goal, Wish, or Challenge. If the answer is no, you may want to consider spending more time developing your Goals, Wishes, or Challenges to match the emotions associated with achieving them.

Continued on 54

Continued from 53

Alive	Delighted	Peaceful
Beautiful	Friendly	Proud
Brave	Generous	Relaxed
Calm	Glad	Relieved
Capable	Great	Respected
Cheerful	Happy	Safe
Comfortable	Joyful	Secure
Confident	Love	Strong

The Invitation

Brushing crumbs off her dress, Greta offered a recommendation to Jack and Jill. "The two of you might benefit from working through CPS with a group. While you can use CPS on your own to solve whatever challenges plague you, groups offer a greater variety and perspective. Groups come in handy when it comes to solving stubborn problems—the type where you might be too close to a problem to objectively find a solution. Groups are also good when you are solving a complex problem—one where you need multidisciplinary thinking and assistance to bring it to life. What do you think about enlisting a group to help you solve your problem?"

"We think it sounds great," sang the twins in unison.

"Wow," said Jack, glancing over at Jill. "I can't believe you agree with me. Let's keep going."

Greta continued, "Okay, then. There are three roles in a group CPS session: the client, the resource group, and the facilitator. You and Jill are the clients, or owners, of the Goal, Wish, or Challenge, and I will serve as the facilitator. My role is to make sure we move through the CPS process successfully. All you need to do now is choose your resource group. The resource group will bring ideas, energy, and new perspective to help you solve your challenge. You should choose resource group members who offer a mix of skills in generating ideas, crafting solutions, clarifying the situation, and getting things done."

"Why is that?" asked Jack. "If what we need is new perspective, why wouldn't we just invite folks who are good at coming up with ideas?"

"You see," answered Greta, "solving problems requires more than just ideas. It takes detective skills to understand what the true problem really is. It takes lots of ideas about how to solve the problem. It takes the ability to connect different ideas and possibilities to create the best solution, and it takes the ability to implement the solution."

"I think I get it," Jack quickly offered. "I suppose with creative problem solving, having diverse skill sets is important. How about including King Cole, and also Cathy Cat and Donny Dog from "Hey Diddle Diddle?"

"Yes," replied Jill. "I like your list. Let's also add Humpty Dumpty."

"What?" questioned Jack.

"You know," started Jill,

"Humpty Dumpty sat on a wall.
Humpty Dumpty had a great fall.
All the king's horses and all the king's men
Couldn't put Humpty back together again."

Jack questioned, "I know Humpty, but w-w-why would we invite the egg? He can't even figure out how to stop falling off the wall! In fact, he doesn't even know our situation. At least King Cole, Cathy, and Donny know what we're going through. They've worked with Greta to change their destinies already."

"True," answered Jill, "but Humpty has found a way to regenerate himself each time he falls. A clever solution, if you ask me. What do you think, Greta?"

Greta replied, "There's a rich reward when you invite folks who are less familiar with your situation. Let's look at an example from people. In 1943, Edwin Land's three-year-old daughter helped him invent the Polaroid camera by asking why she had to wait for the film to be processed. Polaroid became iconic in defining a generation. So, you see, sometimes naïve questions can spur creativity."

"I guess it makes sense to me," said Jack. "I'm starting to see things in a whole new way working with you, Greta. And

Jill, I have to admit you're offering some good suggestions these days. The decision is made. The egg gets an invitation."

"Excellent," chuckled Greta. She urged, "Why don't you send invitations to the resource group inviting them to join you for the CPS session? The king offered his castle as a meeting place. We can schedule the session in a couple of days to give you and Jill enough time to do a small homework assignment."

"Ugh, homework," sighed Jack. "I thought summer was for vacation."

"This is a very simple task," continued Greta. "All you need to do is gather all the data surrounding your challenge. Data goes beyond facts and figures," she explained, handing Jack a worksheet to complete. "Gather all of the artifacts, evidence, and supporting points surrounding your challenge. Then choose the most pertinent. You will use the most pertinent data to paint the challenge for your resource group. Enjoy your homework assignment," she said. "And don't forget to send the invitations to your resource group. I'll meet you both here on Wednesday to review your homework."

"Sounds good," replied Jack. On the walk home, he and Jill penned and delivered an invitation to each participant. *Dear Humpty Dumpty…*"

Chapter 5: Choosing a Resource Group

When it comes to choosing a resource group, it is a good idea to invite individuals who have different creative problem solving preferences. Each of us has our own unique way of being creative. Though there are many creativity assessments, FourSight (www.foursightonline) was developed specifically to identify how each of us is creative. According to the developers of FourSight, people who enjoy asking questions and developing problem statements have Clarifier preferences. Those who enjoy thinking up many ideas or can imagine many possibilities have Ideator preferences. People who enjoy building solutions have Developer preferences. Those who enjoy implementing solutions and getting into action have Implementer preferences. Some people have a combination of preferences. However, it is important to note that it is rare for one person to excel at all four preferences. Because of this, bringing highly creative solutions to life requires

Continued on 62

Continued from 61

bringing many types of creative thinking together. As you can see, teamwork is very important when it comes to creativity and innovation. In fact, it is nearly impossible to solve complex business problems alone.

CHAPTER SIX

Data, Data, Everywhere

Jack and Jill walked into their living room, kicked off their shoes, and gave their mother a big kiss. "Hello, Mom," chirped Jack. "You're not going to believe this, but we're getting really close to conquering the hill. We spent some time with Greta today. She gave us a bit of homework to do to get ready. We'll be on the porch working if you need us."

"Yeah," Jill added, "I'll bet you've never seen us so anxious to do homework before, but this is different. Greta is really amazing. She's guiding us through a problem solving method called CPS. Once we learn CPS, we will finally be able to get down that darned hill. Plus we can apply it to lots of situations throughout our lives. It'll be a great tool for when we start college in the fall."

"Business school isn't going to know what hit them when we walk through the door," chuckled Jack. "There's so much talk about innovation these days, but when you look at the success rate of innovative ideas in business, it's pretty disappointing. Understanding *how* to solve problems creatively will give Jill and me a competitive advantage. And we'll be a million times more valuable to employers. I've been going through the want ads and you wouldn't believe how many companies specify creative problem solving as a required skill. You'll need it for a career in marketing, management, engineering, product design, nursing and education—for that matter, in all industries and on all continents. Just think! By learning CPS, not only will we gain credentials in creativity, but once we conquer the hill, we'll also have tangible results to share."

"How wonderful!" exclaimed the twins' mother. "Maybe you can work on finding a way to pay for college too," she joked. Turning her attention to the bubbling pot on the stove, she continued, "If you need any help, let me know. I think it's wonderful you're working on solving your challenge. And please don't forget you'll need to grab an extra pail on your next trip to the well. We're running a bit low on water since you missed the afternoon run."

"Okay. No problem, Mom!" said Jack. "We'll see you in a bit."

Jack led the way through the house and onto the back porch. While he rearranged the furniture into a small circle, Jill gathered some sticky notes and felt-tip pens. Getting comfortable, Jack pulled out the worksheet Greta had given them.

"Hmm," said Jack, studying the sheet. "Looks like we need to examine our challenge and capture all the relevant data. It says here data includes facts, figures, feelings, curiosities, hunches, and more. Data is a basic: who, what, where, when, why, and how of our challenge. Greta refers to this as 5W's and an H. Pretty good acronym," Jack laughed. "I never counted before but there are 5W's and one H in who, what, where, when, why, and how."

Jill smiled. "Clever, and easy to remember."

"All right," continued Jack, "Greta says we should follow the same format as we did in capturing Goals, Wishes, and Challenges. First, we will diverge—capture all the data on the sticky notes—and then we will converge—choose the most relevant. The sticky notes we end up with after converging will be what we will share with the resource group to bring them up to speed on our challenge. Ready to begin?" he asked his sister.

"Yes," nodded Jill. "Let's do it. We can capture separately and read our sticky notes aloud like we did at Greta's."

With that, the pair began gathering data. Jack captured the following:

> ❄️We've always fallen down the hill. Even before we could walk, Mom and Dad would carry us up the hill. Then, once we fetched the water, our entire family would fall down the hill.

☀ Jill and I have been fetching the water together since we were able to carry the pail.

☀ We use three pails of water per day.

☀ We've tried about a hundred different paths down the hill.

☀ The well is at the top of a craggy hill.

☀ We slip at a different spot every day.

☀ We fall, no matter what time of day we fetch the water.

☀ Sometimes we slip on rocks and twigs; sometimes our laces get caught on branches; sometimes we fall for no reason.

☀ Like everyone in Nursery Rhyme, we dress in the same clothing each day.

And Jill captured these:

☀ Jack always leads the way up and down the hill.

☀ We've tried to conquer the hill by trying many different paths (about a hundred).

☀ It is very important to us to conquer the hill before our eighteenth birthday.

❊ No matter how hard I try, once Jack falls, I tumble, too.

❊ I am frustrated and exasperated by our failure.

❊ Other than trying new paths, we've never tried another way to fetch the water.

❊ We don't have trouble getting up the hill, but always encounter problems coming down the hill.

When they captured all they could, Jack and Jill decided to take a break and continue the exercise after dinner. Greta referred to these types of breaks as incubation. She told the twins that incubation is necessary and helps creativity. Their timing was perfect. As soon as Jack and Jill tidied up the sticky notes, their mom yelled, "Please wash up. It's time for dinner."

The day's work was good for Jack's and Jill's appetite. Each devoured dinner with relish. At the end of the meal, Jack looked at his sister and sighed. "Jill, it's that time again."

"I know, I know," replied Jill sourly. "I was hoping we could put if off for a bit more."

"The faster we fetch the water, the sooner it will be over. Let's just get to it," suggested Jack. "In fact, we can continue data gathering as we're fetching the water. Let's bring the tripod and camera. We can record our efforts for the resource group to see. Since we're behind in fetching the water, the resource group will get to see us fall twice."

"Sure thing," added Jill. "I will bring a backpack too. We can gather samples of the dirt and rocks. It might help the resource group in coming up with ideas."

Jack didn't realize gathering data could be so interesting. He had never taken the time to think about how much depth there was to their challenge. Now that he had stopped to reflect, thinking up different paths and diving head first into action was really tiring. It was becoming a vicious cycle. There did seem to be an underlying benefit in taking time to clarify the problem before coming up with solutions. Now, more than ever, he saw how Jill's way of looking at the world complemented his own way of working. "Different isn't so bad after all," Jack thought to himself.

Minutes later, with the tripod and camera set up at the bottom of the hill, Jack and Jill began their ascent. Jack lowered the pail into the well and hoisted it off the pulley. Nimbly stepping over the bare root of an oak tree, Jack looked into the lens and gave the camera a nod to acknowledge the close call. Unfortunately, a few steps farther, he let out a screech as he slipped on a patch of wet leaves. Hitting the ground with a loud thud, Jack sighed.

Seeing Jack slip, Jill deftly skirted the patch of leaves and clutched a branch to rebalance. However, just at that moment, a cracking sound erupted as the branch tore free from the tree. It was no use! Jill tumbled past Jack and landed twenty yards away.

"All right," said Jack, panting. He looked into the camera and continued, "That was attempt number one." Placing the partially filled pail on the ground, Jack wiped a smear of dirt from his face and continued, "Let's try it again."

This time, at the top of the hill, Jill remembered a thought from the earlier data gathering exercise. "Jack, why don't you hand me the pail and let me lead the way down the hill?" she suggested.

"Why?" asked Jack, suspicious.

"Well, when I was capturing data, it occurred to me you're always the one in the lead. It made me wonder what the outcome would be if I led the way."

"It's worth a try," said Jack, reluctantly, passing Jill the pail.

Unfortunately, even with Jill in the lead, it was no use. The twins still fell down the hill. "I was hopeful that would work," sighed Jack, while picking dried leaves out of his hair and handing them to Jill. "Here are the terrain samples you were looking for. Let me put them into your backpack, and then we can capture additional data from our visit to the hill."

After settling the sample into the backpack, Jack and Jill captured additional data:

> ☀ Even when Jill leads the way, we still fall.

> ☀ Wet leaves and a weak branch caused our fall this time.

> ☀ We want to do away with all the pain. The bumps and bruises are unbearable.

> ☀ We are mentally and physically exhausted from fetching the water.

> ☀ Because it takes us three tries to fetch enough water for the day, we do not have a lot of time to do all the things we would love to do.

> ☀ Since we've never altered the hill, we have a hunch that we may need to do something about the hill in order to stop falling.

From there, Jack and Jill combined all of the Data Gathering sticky notes and chose the most relevant data to share with the resource group. Jack also packed up the video and dropped it into the pack. On the walk home, he pondered, "Jill, I hope Greta can use the video in our session. It might give everyone ideas for helping us solve our problem."

"That sounds like a good idea," responded Jill.

"Really?" asked Jack. "You never think I have good ideas. What's the difference this time?"

Jill responded thoughtfully, "Ever since Greta mentioned problem solving involves many forms of creativity, including coming up with ideas, asking questions, developing solutions, and implementing, I realized the benefit of teamwork and the benefit of ideas."

"Interesting," replied Jack. "I've been thinking about this, too. What I've noticed is we have been getting along really well today. I feel like I understand you a little better. CPS is bringing out the best in each of us. What a nice byproduct of creative problem solving."

SIDEBAR

Chapter 6: 5W's and an H

☀ Who is involved with the situation?

☀ Who makes the decisions?

☀ Who might benefit from fixing the situation?

☀ What happened? (What's the story?)

☀ What have you tried?

☀ What successes have you had?

☀ What challenges have you encountered?

☀ Where did it take place?

☀ Where have you found help?

☀ When did it happen?

☀ Why did it happen?

☀ Why is this a concern?

☀ How did it happen?

☀ How do you feel about the situation?

Chapter 6: Data Gathering

Diverge

☀ Review the Goal, Wish, or Challenge you chose in chapter five.

☀ Capture all of the data surrounding the situation using the 5W's and an H as you see fit.

Converge

☀ Review your sticky notes and choose the most relevant data.

Ground Rules and
Statement Starters

A few days later, Jack and Jill pulled together all of their work from the data gathering session and scurried over to Greta's. Jack hummed a few bars of "Humpty Dumpty" as he led the way through the sunny forest. The warm, calm day set the stage for the twins' meeting.

Spying the little cottage at a distance, Jack yelled out, "Race you to Greta's."

Running full tilt toward the cottage, the twins arrived out of breath. "Hel-llo, Gre-ta!" they gasped.

"Hello," replied Greta. Her wide smile let Jack and Jill know she was genuinely happy to see them. "How did you do with the data gathering homework assignment?" Greta asked.

"It was wonderful," answered Jack.

Greta reviewed all of the rich data Jack and Jill captured. "What an impressive amount of data. I particularly love the video and the dirt, leaf, and rock samples. We will definitely include these artifacts in the CPS session."

Jack was ecstatic. It was as if he was grinning from head to toe. As Jack thought about his experience with King Cole and Greta, he realized how important each of them had become in helping him attain his goal. Jack's quasi-pessimistic attitude about conquering the hill had given way to optimism. The tips, tricks, and guidance Greta provided helped him see the future was bright and full of opportunities.

"Okay, now, let's cover some quick ground rules," said Greta. "We'll take care of this today, so that we don't need to go into detail the day of the CPS session. Since most of the folks in your resource group have participated in a CPS session before, they are familiar with the rules."

"Wow," said Jack. "It is still hard for me to believe King Cole, Cathy and Donny have done this before. I'm beginning to feel as if I've been living in a cave."

"Not necessarily," replied Greta. "Everything is as it should be. Perhaps it just wasn't your time. You may not have been ready to embrace CPS until now. So, this could be *the* perfect time for you. All right," she started, "we spoke earlier about divergence—thinking up—and convergence—choosing a direction. In each step of the CPS process we've completed so far, we've diverged and converged. We'll continue this pattern in the upcoming steps, too."

"Interesting," observed Jack. "Diverging and converging is like a bird flying. A bird needs to raise her wings up, reaching for possibilities, and lower her wings down, gathering the most promising, in order to fly."

"Excellent," said Greta. "You're catching on." With that, she pulled out a sheet with the ground rules for diverging and converging, which read:

Rules for Diverging:

☀ Keep an open mind. Whatever idea comes to mind, go with it. Don't evaluate ideas while you're generating them.

☀ Go for quantity. The more ideas you have, the greater the chances of getting a good one.

☀ Seek unusual ideas. Ideas can get watered down as they are implemented. Going for unusual ideas preserves novelty.

☀ Grow ideas. Piggyback and build upon ideas.

Rules for Converging:

☀ Be positive. Think in terms of "what's good about it?"

☀ Choose the best fit. Check your original goal to make sure there is alignment.

☀ Strengthen ideas. Take time to make your ideas better.

☀ Consider novelty. Don't dismiss original thinking out of hand.

"Let me get something straight," said Jack, turning to Greta. "When we first met with you to come up with Goals, Wishes, and Challenges, we diverged and converged. Then, when we gathered data, we did the same. You mentioned earlier each step of the process includes diverging and converging. So, to use the bird analogy, we will raise our wings and lower our wings at each step and by doing so, we will fly the distance toward attaining our goal."

"That is absolutely correct," smiled Greta. Patting Jack on the back, she asked, "Is it okay if I borrow your analogy and attribute it to you when I use it? It is really one of the best metaphors I've heard. The way you've described diverging and converging is perfect for thinking about CPS."

"Of course you can borrow the analogy!" Jack said enthusiastically.

Jill cautioned, "Okay, Greta, Jack doesn't need any more encouragement. His ego is big enough as it is. What's the next step?"

Chuckling, Greta replied, "Now it's time for statement starters."

"We used statement starters for our Goals, Wishes, and Challenges, right?" asked Jack.

"Yes, you did," responded Greta. "Statement starters are used to promote open-minded thinking. By using open-ended questions, you free your mind to believe that a problem can be solved. It is the difference between saying 'I can't pass the test' and asking 'What might be all the ways I can pass the test?' The first statement closes your mind to possibilities while the open-ended question sets your mind to believing the task is possible. Open-ended questions help set the stage for generating ideas on all the ways to pass the test."

"That's pretty cool," said Jack excitedly. "I can totally see how that would work." He took a copy of the statement starter tip sheet from Greta and read it.

Statement Starters:

Phases in the CPS process are accompanied by particular statement starters. The abbreviations, for when you are writing and need to use shorthand, are included in parentheses.

☀ Identify Goal, Wish, or Challenge

"I wish…" (IW)

"It would be great if…" (IWBGI)

☀ Clarify the Problem

"How to…" (H2)

"How might…" (HM)

"In what ways might…" (IWWM)

"What might be all the…" (WMBAT)

☀ Select and Strengthen Solutions

"What I see myself (us) doing is…" (WISMD)

"Breaking down the CPS process is helping me understand what we'll go through during the session tomorrow," said Jack. "But with all of these rules and ways to phrase statements, I'm getting confused. How will I keep track of everything?"

Greta replied reassuringly, "Jack, it will all come with time. CPS is new to you. As a first-timer, all you need to do is trust the process. I will be here to guide you through each of the steps. As you become familiar with CPS, you will find it as effortless as breathing. CPS was created based on how the human mind naturally works. Think of CPS as a shortcut. Rather than allowing your mind to wander off, CPS provides a simple, repeatable process to get to a better solution more quickly."

"That makes me feel better," said Jack. "The process seems a little foreign at first, but I am sure in time, CPS will become second nature. I guess we just need to practice. If we make CPS a part of our daily lives, I'm sure it will become easier. A simple thing like changing how we pose questions can make a big difference. And I feel like we're already making big strides. Just understanding how Jill and I are creative has helped us get along better."

"That's wonderful," replied Greta as she reviewed Jack and Jill's data gathering assignment. "Your homework is perfect. Now, why don't you head home and rest up for your big day tomorrow?" she suggested.

So, What's the Problem?

So, What's the Problem?

As Jack and Jill crossed the moat to King Cole's castle, Jack felt his heart beating faster in anticipation of conquering the hill. With the days slipping away in the countdown to his eighteenth birthday, today had to be the day that would forever change his life. Stepping into the grand ballroom, Jack smiled as he saw his friends from Nursery Rhyme who had gathered to help him conquer the hill.

After greeting King Cole, Cathy Cat, Donny Dog, and Humpty Dumpty, Jack took in the sights. The ballroom had been transformed into a wonderful problem solving workspace. The shades on the windows were opened wide to let in the light. There were sticky notes galore. The chairs were arranged in a comfortable circle, creating an intimate conversation space. And the tables held a vast array of the terrain samples. Greta had even set up the video alongside a mountain of snacks and beverages. Everything the team needed was in the room. There were even stacks of modeling clay, toys, and curiosities to help get their creative juices flowing.

Seeing that the twins had arrived and settled in, Greta welcomed everyone to the day's activities. She walked the team through a warm-up exercise to help them practice problem finding. She began by showing the team a picture of a gloomy-looking tiger sitting in a rowboat in the middle of a lake. Upon seeing the picture, Jack chuckled, "That's silly. Why would a tiger be in a rowboat in the middle of a lake?"

Greta replied, "A good question, Jack. Also a nice introduction to our warm-up exercise. I would like each of you to study the picture carefully. In opening your mind to all of the possibilities, I would like you to practice thinking up problem statements. Using the statement starters, think up as many problem statements as possible. Write each problem statement on an individual sticky note. What are all the problems you see in this picture? To build some energy, I'm going to have you read your problem statements aloud after you've captured them on the sticky notes."

"Excellent," said Jack. Soon the markers began to squeak as the team feverishly scribbled problem statements.

King Cole was the first to capture a problem statement. He read, "How might the tiger row to shore?"

Jack added, "What might be all the ways the tiger can find happiness?"

Jill piped up, "In what ways might the tiger find his way home?"

After about three minutes, the team began losing steam and the problem statements started slowing down. To help stretch the thinking, Greta suggested, "We have collected a great number of problem statements. Wonderful job! Now, let's stretch a little. Let's think about other perspectives. Who else might be involved? What are other perspectives?" She gave the team a moment to ponder her directions.

Jack was the first to chime in. "I have a problem statement. How might the tiger's friends join him in the row boat?"

"Good one, Jack," said Donny. "I piggybacked on yours. How to make rowing a social sport?"

And so they continued. Jack's eyes widened as he looked up and saw the sea of sticky notes. When all was said and done, the team had captured over thirty problem statements. The problem, which had started out as finding a way to row to shore, quickly expanded to include friends and creating a social endeavor. Although Jack had been through the problem-finding activity just a few days prior, he couldn't help but marvel at all the angles and perspectives one could take in defining a problem.

Now that the warm-up activity was complete, and the team had practiced problem finding, Greta turned the floor over to

Jack. He introduced the team to the twins' Goal, Wish, or Challenge. Jack began, "In thinking about what we would like to accomplish, we've defined our wish as: 'It would be great if we found a safer, more effective way to fetch the water.'"

After anxiously sharing why achieving the goal was so important, Jack and Jill sifted through all the relevant data surrounding the challenge:

- We've always fallen down the hill.

- We use three pails of water per day.

- We've tried about a hundred different paths down the hill.

- The well is at the top of a craggy hill.

- Other than trying new paths, we've never tried another way to fetch the water.

- We never have any trouble getting up the hill, but always encounter problems going down the hill.

- We are mentally and physically exhausted from fetching the water.

- Since we've never altered the hill, we have a hunch that we may need to do something about the hill in order to stop falling.

As Jack and Jill provided rich context to their challenge, King Cole, Cathy, Donny, and Humpty started capturing problem statements just like Greta had taught them in the warm up. They concentrated on what Jack and Jill were saying, scrutinized all the details, and posed open-ended questions based on what they were hearing and inferring. The problem statements included:

- How might Jack and Jill change their destinies?
- In what ways might Jack and Jill change their attitudes about the challenge?
- How might they find another source for water?
- What might be all the ways to clear the debris from the hill?
- How might Jack and Jill fetch a greater amount of water in a single trip?
- How to find better shoes?

☀ In what ways might Jack and Jill enlist help from friends in Nursery Rhyme?

☀ How might Jack and Jill accept their fate?

☀ In what ways might we use solutions for transporting water from the world of people?

☀ How to stop tumbling down the hill?

☀ What might be all the ways to get more traction?

☀ How to fetch water without having to go down the hill?

☀ In what ways might Jack and Jill conquer the hill?

☀ How to get down the hill without falling?

By the time Jack and Jill had finished sharing the data, the resource group had captured over a dozen problem statements. Each took turns reading out problem statements. As they did so, those who were not reading aloud built on the problem statements and captured others. Humpty added:

☀ How to not use water?

☀ How might Jack and Jill get down the hill without falling?

☀ How to fetch water with less effort?

Hearing Humpty's problem statements, Donny continued:

☀ How to hire someone to fetch the water?

☀ What might be all the ways to move water?

☀ What might be all the ways to level the hill?

With the final push for problem statements, Jack, Jill, and the resource group added:

☀ What might be all the ways to manufacture water?

☀ How to bring water to Jack and Jill rather than Jack and Jill to the water?

☀ In what ways might we build a permanent, safe path down the hill?

☀ How to take away the pain?

☀ How to modify the shape of the hill?

☀ How might we hire a guide to lead the way down the hill?

☀ What might be all the substitutes for water?

☀ How to invent a new process for fetching water?

☀ How might we pay someone to fetch water for us?

☀ What might be all the ways to cut back water usage?

After scanning the list of problem statements, Jack was surprised to see the team had captured thirty problem statements. Jack recalled his first conversation with the king. Now he knew what King Cole meant when he said the biggest hurdle to solving a problem can be determining the exact problem to solve. Jack sighed. In looking over all of the problem statements, his head began to spin. Greta suggested it might be a good time for a break. Jack and Jill moved outside and sat under a shady tree to discuss the morning so far.

Jack started, "I can't believe how much we've accomplished in so little time. We've been able to look at the problem from so many more perspectives in the last half hour than we've been able to in seventeen years."

"I know," replied Jill. "I thought I was pretty good at asking questions, but the fact we captured so many problem statements is mind-boggling."

"Yes," continued Jack. "Now we need to figure out what to do with them all. It does seem many of the problem statements are related. When we converge, it should be easier to see how all the problem statements are connected. Plus, we'll be able to look at the clusters of problem statements and determine which ones are symptoms and which ones are root causes."

"What do you mean?" asked Jill.

"Well, take the problem statement 'How to find better shoes?' We wouldn't need better shoes if we could stop falling down the hill. So, if we solved for better shoes, it still might not help us in the long run. Also, it is a solution masking as a problem."

"I get it," smiled Jill. "If we've come this far, it's in our best interest to solve the root of the problem. This will make our efforts more effective and efficient. Can you imagine how much money and frustration we can save by clarifying problems when we get into the working world?"

With a burst of energy from the sunshine and the eye-opening conversation, Jack sang out, "Absolutely. Now, let's head back in and find that pesky problem! There are a lot of problem statements to work with. Where should we start?"

Back inside, Greta began, "Is there one problem statement that stands head and shoulders above the rest in helping you reach your goal of finding a safer, more effective way to fetch the water?"

While rubbing his temples, Jack scanned the problem statements. "Hmm, not really," he replied. "I guess we should start putting the problem statements into order." He began grouping the problem statements into categories, but soon lost focus. Jack knew that while converging was mind-numbing for him, it gave Jill a great deal of energy. He beckoned to Jill and she gladly stepped in to help.

Watching the two instinctively grouping the problem statements, Greta offered some words of encouragement. "Bravo, Jack and Jill! Continue identifying the best problem statements and clustering them into groups. Once you've finished grouping, identify one sticky note in each group to represent that category, or create a problem statement to best represent the grouping."

Jack and Jill nodded in acknowledgment while continuing to work intently. On a few occasions, the twins became stuck and asked King Cole, Cathy, Donny, and Humpty to help talk through the best fit. When all was said and done, Jack and Jill boiled the list of problem statements into six categories:

1. How might we change ourselves?

2. In what ways might we change the hill?

3. What might be all the alternative sources of water?

4. How to conserve water?

5. How to enlist help from others?

6. What might be all the ways to move water?

With a more manageable categorization of problem statements, Jack turned his attention back to their original Goal, Wish, or Challenge. He read, "It would be great to find a safer, more effective way to fetch the water."

Keeping their wish in mind, Jack and Jill talked through the categories of problem statements to figure out which one would best help them achieve their wish. Jack and Jill remembered Greta's recommendation to choose problem statements where you have ownership, motivation, and the need for imagination. After a brief dialogue, the twins decided there was not a big need for imagination to solve categories 1, 4, or 5.

Jack piped up, "While changing ourselves, conserving water, and enlisting help from others may become a part of our final solution, they don't require as much imagination or new thinking as the others." With the list of problem statements growing shorter, Jack and Jill dug into changing the hill, finding alternative sources for water, and ways to move water. In talking about these three, the twins were most motivated to find ways to move water. They put a star on category six and turned to Greta for instruction.

"Great job working through all of the problem statements!" she observed. "It looks like you've chosen to go forward with: 'What might be all the ways to move water.' That's a pretty broad statement. Let's see if we can make it more specific. That will help you focus."

Jack responded, "What if we restate the problem statement as: 'What might be all the ways to move water from the hill to our home?' Would that work?"

"Absolutely," said Greta. "That is better. Now we're ready to start generating ideas."

"I can't wait," squealed Jack. "Generating ideas is going to be my favorite part of CPS. We're getting closer and closer to accomplishing our goal. I can feel it."

"That's interesting, Jack," responded Jill. "It seems to me what you enjoy is diverging—not necessarily just coming up with ideas. You were pretty enthusiastic about thinking up problem statements too."

So, What's the Problem?

Jack considered what Jill had said and added, "I guess you're right. And it seems to me that you're pretty enthusiastic about converging."

Chapter 8: Clarifying the Problem

Diverge

☀ Review the Goal, Wish, or Challenge you chose in chapter five.

☀ Review the pertinent data from chapter six.

☀ Capture all of the problems by phrasing as open-ended statements. Strive for at least thirty problem statements.

☀ Remember to use "How to…? How might…? In what ways might…? What might be all the ways…?"

Converge

☀ Review your sticky notes and choose the most promising problem statement.

Ideas: Quantity
Drives Quality

"Before we dive into where we are going, let's refresh our memories on where we have been," said Greta. "While CPS does not need to be used as a whole, it seemed best suited for the challenge since your challenge was not well-defined and required us to start with Identifying the Goal, Wish, or Challenge. You chose, 'It would be great to find a safer, more effective way to fetch the water.' Then we defined the key data. Finally, we described the problem statement as 'What might be all the ways to move water from the hill to our home?' We've accomplished so much in such a short time. Thank you for your energy and enthusiasm," she cheered. "Now, does anyone have questions or observations about the CPS process before we begin?"

"I do," said Jack, eagerly raising his hand.

"What would you like to share with us?" asked Greta.

"Well, I see linkages in everything we've done so far." Jack picked up a marker and began to draw. "The problem statement is driven from the key data that is connected to the Goal, Wish, or Challenge. By solving the problem, we will accomplish our goal using all of the data we collected. CPS seems to be a connected and logical process."

"Indeed," said Greta. "Remember, when they were developing the CPS process, Alex Osborn and Sid Parnes spent a great deal of time studying how we instinctively solve problems. The two created a structured method for solving problems based on how our minds work. That makes CPS intuitive and, as you mentioned, connected. Using CPS can help by aligning everyone's efforts toward reaching a common goal—less stress, fewer fits and starts, fewer changes in direction, and fewer good ideas left on the cutting room floor."

Greta continued, "And, CPS can be used as a whole or in parts depending on your specific needs."

Jack took in the gravity of Greta's statement. "Wow!" he said. "This is heavy stuff. Creative problem solving has to be one of the key ingredients in leadership."

"You're getting the picture," Greta said with a wink. "Now, are you ready to spend some time thinking up ideas to solve our problem?" Eyeing Jack, Jill, King Cole, Donny, Cathy, and Humpty sitting on the edges of their seats, Greta continued, "What you'll find is that, after a few minutes, the number of ideas will begin to slow down. Once I see that everyone has been able to capture their initial ideas, I will introduce some activities to help stretch your ideational abilities. Let's begin. We'll use the same process of capturing one idea per sticky note as we have with the first few steps of CPS. Take a good look at the problem statement and start capturing ideas. What ideas do you have for solving the problem?"

Jack could feel his energy rising as he prepared to diverge. He turned the problem statement around in his mind and asked himself, "What might be all the ways to move water from the hill to our home?" The ideas began to flow. As Jack captured ideas, he could feel a tingling, radiating sensation in his brain. It was as if Jack could actually feel each idea being born and the energy as each idea connected with another. Jack began to capture ideas furiously, but neatly, as Greta had instructed. Jack started by thinking about movement and how things get from one place to another. He wrote:

☀ Use wheels to move the water: car, trolley, train, bicycle, pulley system.

☀ Use wind to move the water: kite, wind chimes.

☀ Use gravity to move the water.

☀ Use a hose.

Jill, on the other hand, took another path. She thought about ways ancient people and not-so-ancient people transported water:

☀ Pump the water.

☀ Dig a channel.

☀ Build an aqueduct.

☀ Use pipes.

☀ Build a tunnel.

☀ Re-route the water.

In listening to Jack's and Jill's ideas, King Cole considered the types of machinery that transport water and captured:

☀ Transport water by car.

☀ Transport water by boat.

☀ Transport water by train.

Cathy and Donny turned their focus to nature. That was one of the benefits of being a cat and a dog. They knew a great deal about plants and animals. Cathy and Donny added:

☀ Create a pouch to carry water—like a dew gecko or camel.

☀ Build a circulatory system to transport water—like the human heart.

☀ Create a root system to transport water—similar to plants.

☀ Dig for water—like dingoes and desert elephants.

☀ Conserve water so you have less to move—like kangaroo rats that stay underground in the heat of the day and have special respiratory systems to capture moisture that might otherwise escape from their lungs.

Lastly, Humpty's ability to regenerate himself each time he fell off the wall helped him capture ideas in an entirely different realm. His ideas centered on reusing water:

☀ Collect rainwater.

☀ Reuse water—like using bath water to water the garden.

☀ Recapture the steam that escapes from the pot when cooking.

Seeing that the team was slowing down, Greta counted twenty ideas and determined it was time to provide techniques to help the team strive for quantity. While there are many divergence tools like Famous People, Perspectives, or Visual Connections, the tool she chose was called Idea Swap. Because

Jack, Jill, King Cole, Cathy, Donny, and Humpty each chose different themes for generating ideas, Greta felt it would be beneficial to give everyone time to reflect on one another's ideas and deliberately build upon them.

To prepare for Idea Swap, Greta asked everyone to organize their sticky notes so they were laid out in front of their seats. Then she asked everyone to stand up and switch seats with the person in front of him/her. She then asked Jack, Jill, King Cole, Cathy, Donny, and Humpty to study the sticky notes in front of them. Using the sticky notes as a springboard, Greta asked each participant to build on one another's ideas by adding his/her own ideas to the group. Physically changing seats, effectively changing perspective, and reviewing one another's ideas would ideally result in a flurry of new ideas built from what the team had captured previously.

The team began the Idea Swap activity. Jack swapped seats with King Cole and studied the king's ideas. Picking up where the king left off, Jack's mind continued down the machinery path and then roamed into water delivery and water storage systems. His idea builds included:

⚜ Fly water from the hill to our home.

⚜ Use bicycles to deliver water.

☀ Skateboard water to our home.

☀ Create an escalator system.

☀ Create an alpine slide to get the water down the hill.

☀ Build a water tower.

☀ Create a water factory.

☀ Deliver water to individual homes like the post office delivers the mail.

Jill sat in Cathy and Donny's space. She was fascinated by how Cathy and Donny leveraged nature for ideas on how to solve the problem. However, Jill felt overwhelmed. She didn't feel as qualified as Cathy and Donny to come up with ideas on how to leverage nature.

Watching Jill write down and then cross out ideas, Greta reminded Jill they were in the divergence stage of idea generation and there would be plenty of time for convergence later. Greta suggested, "Jill, when you think up and discard ideas at the same time, things get muddled. Because you aren't allowing all the ideas to get out before you choose, your brain starts to wander in circles, making it easy to lose sight of your goal. Rather than diverging and converging at the same time, remember there are no silly ideas at this point." Pausing, she urged Jill, "Write down whatever comes to mind. Culling down the ideas and choosing the most promising will come with the next step."

That little bit of encouragement was all that Jill needed. Though she preferred converging, Jill stepped outside of her comfort zone and allowed her ideas to see the light of day. She captured:

- Collect the morning dew from the broad leaves.

- Gather snow and blocks of ice in the winter and melt them for water.

- Move the well from the top of the hill to the bottom of the hill as gravity causes water to flow downhill.

- Follow the forest animals to see where they get their water.

In Jill's spot, Cathy and Donny scanned Jill's ideas and considered how people transport water and the simple machines they created to move heavy objects. After all, if the resource group could help Jack and Jill figure out how to actually fetch more water, it would be beneficial to help Jack and Jill carry the heavy load. Cathy and Donny captured:

- Use a lever.

※ Create a pulley system.

※ Build a ramp.

※ Incorporate wheels.

※ Use axles.

The king studied Humpty's ideas. In thinking about recapturing water, he scanned his mind for opportunities in Nursery Rhyme. "There has to be a way to recapture water in Nursery Rhyme. I just know it," the king muttered to himself. Just then, a glimmer of sunlight caught his eye. In the far corner of the room, King Cole found the source of the glimmer. He crouched down and peered thoughtfully at the silky, shiny threads of a spider web. "That's it," he sang out.

Jack looked up. "King Cole, is everything all right?"

"Absolutely," replied King Cole. "I just stumbled upon an idea for recapturing water." He recited under his breath:

"THE ITSY BITSY SPIDER WENT UP THE WATER SPOUT.
DOWN CAME THE RAIN AND WASHED THE SPIDER OUT.
OUT CAME THE SUN AND DRIED UP ALL THE RAIN.
AND THE ITSY BITSY SPIDER WENT
UP THE SPOUT AGAIN."

"We can partner with Sammy Spider to capture the rainwater." With that said, King Cole happily wrote his idea on the sticky note.

Greta was proud of the team. In just a matter of minutes, they had captured many useful ideas. Taking the king's idea of partnering with Sammy Spider as a teaching opportunity, Greta shared an observation. "I just wanted to point out that the creativity technique the king used is called visual connections. The king used his eyesight to spy Sammy in the corner and then created a connection between Jack and Jill's problem to how Sammy could help."

Excited to practice a new tool for coming up with ideas, Jack suggested, "Humpty, let's work together to practice visual connections."

"Sounds great," replied Humpty.

With that, the two thought about Jack's theme of movement and looked outside for inspiration. In the distance they saw children in Nursery Rhyme rolling balls to one another. They connected the theme of movement to children playing and captured:

- ☀ Create a sphere to move the water—like a giant ball you could fill with water and roll easily from place to place.

- ☀ Move the water like you might a hockey puck on ice.

- ☀ Construct a slide to easily glide water down the hill.

Before long, the team had gone from twenty ideas to over forty. As Jack and Jill scanned all of the ideas, they concluded there were a handful of ideas that stood head and shoulders above the rest. So, rather than going through the exercise of Hits and Clustering, the twins dashed for their felt-tip markers and starred the ideas that provided the best chance for solving their challenge.

"Let's see," began Jack, "I really love the theme of nature." With the felt-tip marker in hand, he continued, "There's something about using gravity, conserving water, reusing water, and collecting naturally falling rainwater that is very compelling." Jack starred the corresponding sticky notes:

☀ Use gravity to move the water.

☀ Conserve water so you have less to move—like kangaroo rats that stay underground in the heat of the day and have special respiratory systems that capture moisture that might otherwise escape from their lungs.

☀ Collect rainwater.

☀ Reuse water—like using bathing water to water the garden.

☀ Create a pouch to carry water—like a dew gecko or camel.

☀ Move the well from the top of the hill to the bottom of the hill as gravity causes water to flow downhill.

☀ Create an alpine slide to get water down the hill.

☀ Partner with Sammy Spider to capture the rainwater.

"Yes," replied Jill, "Very eco-friendly, sustainable, and fantastic solutions at the same time. I also like the idea of finding easier ways to move the water. There's something intriguing about the ease with which a ball rolls that could be useful for us." She placed a star on the sticky note that said,

'Create a sphere to move the water—like a giant ball you could fill with water and roll easily from place to place.'

With the convergence complete, Jack took stock of all the wonderful ideas and eagerly anticipated the last two steps of the process.

Chapter 9: Creativity Techniques

Stuck for new ideas? Give these creativity techniques a whirl.

Famous People

Think about the situation from a famous person's point of view and develop ideas based on his/her way of thinking. For example, how might George Washington, Charlie Brown, Betsy Ross, or your favorite actor think about your situation? What ideas might he or she give you?

Perspectives

Consider who else is involved in the situation. For example, Jack and Jill might consider the perspective of the person who owns the land on which the well is situated or they might consider the citizens of Nursery Rhyme. What might these people think about the situation? What ideas might they provide?

Continued on 119

Continued from 118
Visual Connections

Many of us are visual thinkers. This means we learn best by using our sight. Grab a magazine or look around you, and choose an image that is interesting—one that speaks positively to you. Focus on what you're seeing in the picture and what you're feeling. Write down at least four observations about the picture. Now, using the observations of the picture, think about your problem statement. What ideas does this give you for solving your problem?

Chapter 9: Generating Ideas

Diverge

※ Review the Goal, Wish, or Challenge you chose in chapter five.

※ Review your pertinent data from chapter six.

※ Review the Problem Statement you chose from chapter eight.

※ Capture all the ideas you can to solve your problem. Strive for at least thirty. If you get stuck, try one of the creativity techniques.

Converge

※ Review your sticky notes and choose the most promising ideas.

Developing
the Solution

"Very well," cheered Greta. "A great start indeed. Now, let's pull the solution into a statement that captures what you see yourselves doing." Crossing the room, Greta taped a number of poster-sized blank pages to the wall. At the top of the first sheet she wrote, "What we see ourselves doing is…"

She continued, "The next step is to outline all the activities you see yourselves doing in order to implement your solution. Your description should be detailed enough so that someone who isn't familiar with your challenge can pick up your description and fully understand what you have in mind. Feel free to use as much space as you need to capture the solution. At this stage, it is best to describe the dickens out of the solution so that you do not leave any stone unturned. Helping folks who were not in the room today understand why you've chosen these particular ideas will build support for your solution as you bring it to life."

"Okay," said Jack. "I get it. All we need to do is take all of the most promising ideas, fill in the details, and pull them together to form the solution. Jill, what do you think? Any questions before we get started?"

Jill replied, "Actually, Jack, I do have one question. Thank you for asking. My question is: Do we form our solution based only on the ideas we just captured or can we take a look at all of the sticky notes we've captured so far?"

Greta chimed in, "I'll field that question. You can absolutely go back and take a look at all of the sticky notes we've written during our session. And if you have thoughts for a solution that haven't been captured yet, feel free to write them down. Now that we're nearing the end of the process, it is always useful to review all that we've done in order to build a robust solution," she finished.

"Excellent!" said Jack, pacing. "I'll get us started, Jill. You can fill in anything I miss." Looking back and forth from the starred sticky notes to the blank sheets of poster-sized paper, Jack jotted the following:

What we see ourselves doing is conserving water by not keeping it running when we brush our teeth or when we rinse the dishes. We will reuse water from our daily activities, like using bath water to irrigate the garden. We will also collect rainwater in rain barrels and by partnering with Sammy the Spider. To make it easier to fetch the water, we will relocate the well from the top of the hill to the bottom of the hill. This will prevent us from falling. Also, we will construct a giant-sized rubber ball (like the big exercise balls people use for yoga) to transport the water from the bottom of the hill to our home. By using a rubber ball rather than pails, we should be able to fetch enough water in one trip so that we have more time for fun. Other benefits of using the rubber ball include mobility (easy to roll a ball down the hill), storage (easy to store the rubber ball as it will collapse when it is not full of water), and cost (the rubber ball should be inexpensive to manufacture).

Pausing for a moment to take in the solution, Jack turned to Jill and asked, "Say, what do you think about using our new solution to help pay for college?"

Jill replied quizzically, "I love it. But I'm not sure I follow you."

With that, Jack wrote, "And lastly, we see ourselves starting a water delivery service for the citizens of Nursery Rhyme to help defray the cost of our education."

"That's it," clapped Jill. "We've done it! What a brilliant solution to our challenge."

As King Cole, Cathy, Donny, Humpty, Jack, Jill, and Greta gathered around the newly written solution to absorb the momentous accomplishment, a burst of energy propelled the team onto the final step.

Chapter 10: Developing the Solution

Diverge

❊ Review the Goal, Wish, or Challenge you chose in chapter five.

❊ Review the pertinent data from chapter six.

❊ Review your problem statement from chapter eight.

❊ Evaluate and strengthen your most promising ideas from chapter nine.

Converge

❊ Bring your most promising ideas together to form a solution statement.

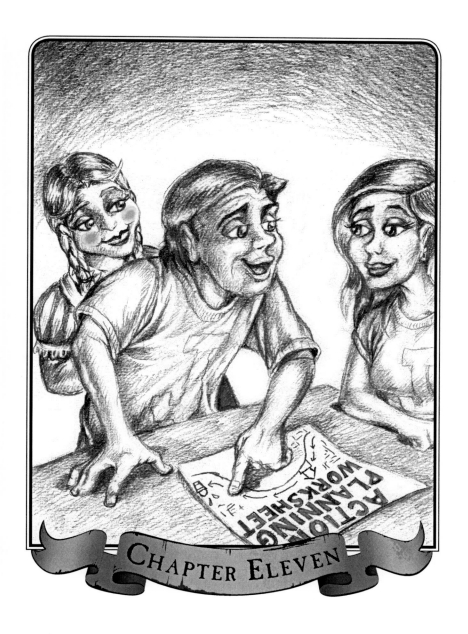

CHAPTER ELEVEN

Getting into Action

"Well, we are nearing the end," said Greta. "The last activity we must embark upon is planning for action. To do so, all you need to do is think about the solution you've defined and list the action steps that will need to be taken in order to bring the solution to life along with dates by which the activities will be complete."

"No worries," said Jack. "That's easy."

"Hold on," interrupted Jill. "What if Jack and I are not able to bring the solution to life by ourselves? For example, we don't know how to relocate a well."

"Good question," responded Greta. "When you list the activities it is fair to assume you will not complete every one of them on your own. You and Jack are more like managers of this project. You will be responsible for identifying and bringing the best team together to help you."

"Perfect," said Jill. "Thank you for the clarification."

"I have an idea for how to relocate the well," sang Jack. The opportunity to diverge, create ideas, and make connections unlocked another burst of energy. "We know a construction crew who can help."

"We do?" Jill asked skeptically.

"Yes, we do," Jack replied smugly.

"LONDON BRIDGE IS FALLING DOWN,

FALLING DOWN, FALLING DOWN.

LONDON BRIDGE IS FALLING DOWN,

MY FAIR LADY..."

"Yes, you're right," exclaimed Jill. "The London Bridge construction crew can definitely help."

With that bit of encouragement, Jack studied the action planning worksheet that Greta had placed in front of him. He and Jill captured action items, responsible parties, and completion dates.

Action Item	Responsible	Completion Date
Conserve water at home	Jack and Jill	Start tomorrow morning
Reuse water from daily activities	Jack and Jill	Start tomorrow morning
Buy rain barrels	Jack	Tomorrow afternoon
Speak to Sammy Spider about a partnership	Jack	Monday, when Sammy is back from vacation
Begin collecting rainwater	Jack	Each time it rains

Action Item	Responsible	Completion Date
Talk to the London Bridge construction crew about what it will take to move the well from the top of the hill to the bottom of the hill	Jack and Jill	Wednesday
Secure equipment, supplies, team, permits, and other items to prepare for moving the well	London Bridge	To be determined upon speaking with the construction crew
Set up a conversation with Olivia, the old woman who lived in a shoe	Jack and Jill	Wednesday
Construct a prototype for the rubber ball	Olivia	To be determined upon speaking with Olivia
Choose the best prototype to manufacture	Jack and Jill	To be determined upon speaking with Olivia
Determine the number of citizens in Nursery Rhyme who want water delivery service	King Cole	Two Thursdays from now
Manufacture rubber balls	Olivia	To be determined upon speaking with Olivia
Talk to the Muffin Man about delivering water along with his home delivery of muffins	Jack and Jill	Friday

After completing the action worksheet, Jack shared his thinking for why they chose Olivia, the old woman who lived in a shoe, to help manufacture the rubber ball. "It's simple,"

Jack began. "If she can fashion a house out of a shoe for all of her children to live in, I'm sure she'll be able to help us construct a simple rubber ball. She's quite resourceful."

Taking a step back and looking over the action list, Jack could hardly believe he and Jill had solved their problem. The generosity of Greta, King Cole, Cathy, Donny, and Humpty Dumpty touched his heart. Though a lump had formed in his throat making it difficult to speak, Jack managed to give each member of the problem-solving team a warm hug.

As Jack and Jill made their rounds to say thank you for the team's enormous contribution, Greta reminded them that while they were both well on their way, the problem was not solved yet. She congratulated them on their success so far and urged them to follow through with their action items. Greta shared, "Getting into action early sets the stage for success. Be sure to act on at least one action item within the next twenty-four hours so that you do not lose momentum. And sometimes it helps to have someone to report your progress to. If you'd like, I'd be happy to serve as your coach and check in on how you're doing in completing your action plan."

"That would be fantastic," cheered Jack and Jill.

"Wonderful," answered Greta. "Now, we all have a surprise for the two of you. We were positive you would find a solution to your problem and took the liberty of organizing a party. To celebrate your success in solving your challenge and to celebrate your eighteenth birthdays, King Cole is throwing a lavish feast in your honor. We will gather at the king's castle one month from now so that you'll have time to work through your action list and share how you're doing in changing the ending of your story."

Chapter 11: Planning for Action

Diverge

※ List all the steps you will need to take in order to implement your solution.

Converge

※ Create an action plan including the steps, responsible parties, and estimated completion dates.

CHAPTER TWELVE

Success!

Success!

A month later, Jack and Jill walked into the King Cole's ballroom accompanied proudly by their parents. Jack and Jill had a confident spring in their steps. "Ah, the grand ballroom!" Jack exclaimed. "This is where it all began. We first entered this ballroom distraught and seeking the king's help to conquer the hill. We now return to the ballroom with our friends from Nursery Rhyme to celebrate our success. In a short period of time and with the help of King Cole, Cathy, Donny, Humpty, and most of all, Greta, we accomplished our goal in time for our eighteenth birthday!"

"Yes, it is pretty amazing when you think about it," added Jill. "We learned some really simple yet amazing techniques for solving problems. All we needed to do was trust the process and trust one another. Jack, I've come to understand how your mind works and I better appreciate your ability to think up ideas."

"Hey, you two," waved the king. "It is great to see you. What a difference a short time makes. You both look radiant." Moving to the head of the table, King Cole motioned all of the guests to be seated. He then suggested Jack and Jill kick off the feast by opening their presents.

"This is my kind of party," said Jack. "I love starting with presents first!"

Jill tore open the paper and exclaimed, "Thank you so much. Our very own creative problem solving toolkit complete with sticky notes, felt-tip pens, and instruction booklet! We're going to get a lot of use out of this."

"And," added Jack, "here is a set of divergent thinking cards to help us practice thinking out of the box." Picking up two of the cards, he read, "Bob's Bathtubs is looking to create a new line of bathtubs. What might be all the ways to improve a bathtub?" Continuing, Jack read the second card, "The International Broccoli Growers Association wants to find more ways to get people to eat broccoli. How might you increase consumption of broccoli?" Considering all the possibilities was energizing. Jack smiled. "I love coming up with ideas. If anyone wants to practice catch me after the feast."

Jill exclaimed, "We also received a captivating set of photographs that we can use to make visual connections and extend our imaginations."

This is amazing!" said Jack with a tear welling in his eye. "The citizens of Nursery Rhyme have given us magnificent gifts. The only way to truly thank you is to pay it forward. Jill and I have been practicing CPS over the last four weeks and we're going to team up with Greta to help anyone in Nursery

Rhyme who wants to change the ending of his or her story. If you're interested, just add your name to the sign-up sheet."

The room broke out in cries of "Hip, hip, and hooray!" The merriment erupted into all of Nursery Rhyme singing Jack and Jill's new story:

"JACK AND JILL SIDESTEPPED THE HILL TO
FETCH A DAY'S WORTH OF WATER.
THEY FILLED UP THE BALL AND DELIVERED TO ALL
AND, BOTH LIVED HAPPILY AFTER."

In just a short amount of time, Jack and Jill had changed their destinies. As they looked at the sign-up sheet, their hearts swelled at the opportunity to help Humpty Dumpty, Baa Baa Black Sheep, and other friends in Nursery Rhyme change their stories as well.

Chapter 12: Debriefing

Now that you've come to the end of the book, it is time to debrief on what you have learned. Debriefing helps to engage continual learning. Ask yourself:

What?

What did you learn?

So what?

What impact does this have?

What difference does this make?

Now what?

What will you do differently as a consequence?

How will you apply what you learned?

GLOSSARY

5Ws and an H – a creativity technique used during data gathering to identify the who, what, where, when, why, and how.

association of ideas – defined by Alex Osborn as ideas leading to other ideas.

"big-C" creativity – also referred to as transformational creativity. This type of creativity is a more radical type of creativity that comes from moving beyond the conceptual space. An example of big-C creativity is the development of computers.

biomimicry – the science behind copying or mimicking nature to solve problems.

brainstorming – a group creativity technique for coming up with a large number of ideas to a problem.

Clarifier – a FourSight term to identify people who have preferences for asking questions and developing problem statements.

Clarifying the Problem – a step in CPS where you use the statement starters "How to…?" "How might…?" In what ways might…?" What might be all the ways…?" to identify and hone in on the problem to be solved.

client –the owner of the Goal, Wish, or Challenge. In this story there are two clients, Jack and Jill.

converge – to bring together, or to choose the most promising.

CPS – an acronym for the Osborn-Parnes Creative Problem Solving Process.

Developer – a FourSight term to identify people who have preferences for building solutions.

Developing Solutions – a step in CPS where you identify the most promising ideas and strengthen and combine them to form a solution statement. Solution statements begin with the phrase, "What I/we see myself/ourselves doing is…"

diverge – to branch out, or seek many possibilities.

Glossary

facilitator – guides the team through the CPS process.

Gathering Data – refers to a step in CPS where you identify facts, figures, feelings, curiosities, and hunches surrounding the situation.

Generating Ideas – a step in CPS where you consider the problem statement and capture many ways to solve it.

higher order wish – a wish that, if attained, helps to achieve all the other wishes.

Hits and Clustering – a creativity technique used for converging. To practice, "Hit" or identify the pertinent information, then "Cluster" or group by theme.

Ideator – a FourSight term to identify people who have preferences for thinking up many ideas or imagining many possibilities.

Identifying the Goal, Wish, or Challenge – using the statement starters "I wish…" and "It would be great if…" to define the topic for CPS.

imagination – testing for imagination involves asking if you really want to bring novel thinking to the situation.

Implementer – a FourSight term to identify people who have preferences for implementing solutions and getting into action.

"little-c" creativity – also referred to as everyday creativity. This type of creativity is what we see around us on a daily basis. An example of little-c creativity is combining chocolate and peanut butter to make a new recipe.

motivation – testing for motivation involves asking if you really want to take action on a particular issue.

Osborn-Parnes Creative Problem Solving Process – also known as CPS. A simple, repeatable way to bring new thinking to challenges. Steps in the process include Identifying the Goal, Wish, or Challenge; Gathering Data; Clarifying the Problem; Generating Ideas; Developing Solutions; and Planning for Action.

ownership – testing for ownership involves asking if you are responsible for the situation.

piggybacking – implies building upon a thought, idea, or notion.

Planning for Action – a step in CPS where you list out action steps, responsible parties, and completion dates for each item that needs to be addressed in order to bring your solution to life.

positive emotions – help set the tone for creativity.

problem statement – open-ended questions used during the Clarify the Problem step. Statement starters begin with "How to...?" "How might...?" "In what ways might...?" "What might be all the ways...?"

relevant data – a term for identifying the most pertinent data during the convergence phase of Data Gathering.

resource group – invited by the client and bring ideas, energy, and new perspective to help solve the challenge. In choosing resource group members, it is best to look to those who offer a mix of skills in generating ideas, crafting solutions, clarifying the situation, and getting things done.

sticky notes – slips of paper that temporarily stick to documents or surfaces. In CPS, participants use sticky notes during each of the steps to capture Goals, Wishes, and Challenges, Data, Problem Statements, Ideas, Solution Statements, and Action Planning items. Because sticky notes can be moved around, they make diverging and converging easier. Sticky notes are recyclable too!

strengthening – building upon a concept in order to make it better.

visual connection – a creativity technique used for diverging.

wish making – refers to the act of Identifying Goals, Wishes, or Challenges.

BIBLIOGRAPHY

Arnold, A. (2010, Spring). Creativity and gifted education: Seeing the forest and the trees. *Newsletter of the NAGC Creativity Network, 6*(1), pp. 12-13.

Arnold, A. (2010). Building a creative organization. *Bloomberg Businessweek.* Retrieved from http://www.businessweek.com/managing/content/sep2010/ca2010091_968396.htm

Bagley, K. *Natural forms of flattery.* Retrieved January 31, 2011, from http://audubonmagazine.org/web/biomimicry/

Bellis, M. *History of flight – The Wright brothers.* Retrieved January 31, 2011, from http://inventors.about.com/od/wstartinventors/a/TheWrightBrother.htm

Capitalizing on complexity: Insights from the global chief executive officer study." *IBM Institute for Business Value.* May 2010.

Csikszentmihalyi, M. (2008). *Flow: The psychology of optimal experience*. New York: Harper Perennial Modern Classics.

Erren, T. C. (2009). On gestational periods of creative work: An interface of Doig's art and science. *Medical Hypotheses, 74*, 4-6.

Fishkin, A. S., & Johnson, A. S. (1998). Who is creative? Identifying children's creative abilities. *Roeper Review, 21*(1), 40

Instant Photogrpahy. Retrieved January 31, 2011, from http://www.rowland.harvard.edu/organization/land/ instantphoto.php

Isaksen, S., &Treffinger, D. (2004). Celebrating 50 years of Reflective Practice: Versions of Creative Problem Solving. *Journal of Creative Behavior, 38*(2), 75-101. Retrieved May 18, 2009, from Education Research Complete database.

Keller-Mathers, S., & Pagliaroli, A. (2010). Creative learning, thinking and problem solving: 21st century partner in education. *Pennsylvania Educational Leadership, 29*(1), 24-31.

Bibliography

Miller, B., Vehar, J., Firestien, R. (2001). *Creativity Unbound: An introduction to creative process* (3rd ed.). Williamsville, NY: Innovation Resources, Inc.

Miller, B., Vehar, J., Firestien, R. (2001). *Facilitation: A door to creative leadership* (3rd ed.). Williamsville, NY: Innovation Resources, Inc.

Osborn, A. F. (1963). *Applied imagination* (3rd ed.). New York: Charles Scribner's Sons.

Osborn, A. F. (1964). *How to become more creative: 101 rewarding ways to develop your potential talent.* New York: Charles Scribner's Sons.

Osborn, J. (2004). Biography: Alex F. Osborn. *Journal of Creative Behavior, 38*(1), 70-72. Retrieved May 18, 2009, from Education Research Complete database.

Osborn, A. F. (2009). *Your creative power: How to use your imagination to brighten life, to get ahead.* (Rev. ed.). Maryland: Hamilton Books.

Parnes, S. J., (Ed.). (1992). *Source book for creative problem solving: A fifty year digest of proven innovation processes.* Buffalo, NY: Creative Education Foundation Press.

Puccio, G. J. (2002). Foursight: The breakthrough thinking profile. Retrieved from http://www.foursightonline.com/dojo/4/manual.pdf

Puccio, G. J. & Grivas, C. (2009). Examining the relationship between personality traits and creativity styles. Creativity and Innovation Management, *18*(4), 247- 255.

Puccio, G. J., Murdock, M. C., & Mance, M. (2007). *Creative leadership: Skills that drive change.* Thousand Oaks, CA: Sage Publications.

Puccio, G. J., & Murdock, M. C. (2007).*Creativity assessment: Readings and resources.* Hadley, MA: The Creative Education Foundation Press.

Roberts, R. M. (1989). *Serendipity: Accidental discoveries in science.* New York: John Wiley & Sons, Inc.

Robinson, K. & Aronica, L. (2009). *The element: How finding your passion changes everything.* New York: Viking.

Ross, P. O. (1993). National excellence: A case for developing America's talent. Retrieved November 21, 2007 from http://www.ed.gov/pubs/DevTalent/intro.html

Bibliography

Torrance, E. P., & Sisk, D. A. (2001), *Gifted and talented children in the regular classroom*. Buffalo, NY: Creative Education Foundation Press.

INDEX

AUTHOR BIO

Alicia Arnold holds a Master of Science in Creative Studies from the International Center for Studies in Creativity at Buffalo State College and an MBA in Marketing from Bentley University. She is a certified facilitator of the Osborn-Parnes

Creative Problem Solving Process (CPS) and is an invited presenter at the annual Creative Problem Solving Institute. Alicia has published on the topic of creativity with *Bloomberg Businessweek*, *The National Association of Gifted Children*, and *iMedia Connection*.

Alicia is a creativity scholar and practitioner. In her role as an award-winning digital marketer she uses her passion for creativity and innovation to train teams on creativity techniques, to develop breakthrough digital experiences, and to facilitate CPS workshops. In the workshops, Alicia utilizes nursery rhymes to help clients become comfortable with the CPS process. The positive feedback about the approachability and simplicity of using nursery rhymes as a teaching tool led to the concept for *Creatively Ever After*.

**To learn more, visit www.alicia-arnold.com
or follow Alicia on Twitter at http://twitter.com/alicarnold**

ORDER FORM

To book the author for speaking engagements, seminars,
or training please visit http://alicia-arnold.com

For information about special discounts or for bulk
purchases, contact alderhillpress@gmail.com.

Order Form for 1-5 Copies

Payable in US funds only. Book price $15.95 each copy. Postage and handling
US $4.95 for first book, $1.00 for each additional book; International $5.50 for
one book; $1.00 for each additional book. We accept Visa, MC, AMEX only. No
Cash/COD.

Email orders:
alderhillpress@gmail.com

Postal orders:
Alder Hill Press
P. O. Box 563
Hanover, MA 02339

Bill my credit card _____ Expiration _____

❑ Visa ❑ MC ❑ AMEX   Signature _____

Bill to:

NAME _____

ADDRESS _____

CITY, STATE, ZIP _____

DAYTIME PHONE _____

Ship to:

NAME _____

ADDRESS _____

CITY, STATE, ZIP _____

DAYTIME PHONE _____

*Please allow 4–6
weeks for US
delivery. Can./Int'l
orders please allow
6–8 weeks. This offer
is subject to change
without notice.*

Number of books $ _____

Price $ _____

Book total $ _____

Applicable sales tax $ _____

Postage & Handling $ _____

Total amount due $ _____